Old Age: Idle Thoughts, Recollections

M B NAIR

INDIA · SINGAPORE · MALAYSIA

Copyright © M B Nair 2024
All Rights Reserved.

ISBN 979-8-89475-029-3

Contents

Contents

Preface

As the title indicates, the book contains my thoughts and recollections, thoughts on matters ranging from Bhagavad Geetha to Marxism and recollections of personal experiences.

I have seen saffron-clad '*yogis*' with snow-white beard and matted hair coming out with what they considered as the 'secrets' of Bhagavad Geetha during their *Geetha parayana* (recital of Bhagavad Geetha) meant for 'believers'. I have also seen quite a few persons quoting passages from Bhagavad Geetha and posing as scholars well-versed in Bhagavad Geetha. Such experiences prompted me to read this 'venerated scripture' and find out for myself what it really conveyed.

As a student of Sanskrit, reading and understanding the original text in Sanskrit posed no great problem for me. I had also commentaries on Bhagavad Geetha written by great men like Swamy Vivekananda and Bal Gangadhar Tilak to guide me whenever I got stuck.

Most people are in the habit of looking at Bhagavad Geetha as something sacred. If we approach it in that conventional manner, there is nothing much that we can look for. The first thing a discerning reader ought to do is to take it out of that sanctified pedestal and look at it as the expression of human wisdom,

wisdom of the age in which it was composed and perfected. That approach will help us to weed out what appears incongruous or outdated today and preserve what appears relevant.

Events of the latter half of the last century which have become part of history today were everyday experiences for me. As a student of history, I could relate them to their historical background and put them in their proper perspective. Observations on some of those events circulating these days, I find not only at variance with truth but also deliberately meant to misguide public opinion. That is what provoked me to write on West Asia, China, Marxism and Democracy, coming out with what I feel as the correct version. I made sure that my findings are fact-based and free from personal prejudices.

everyone goes through some experience or the other in life worthy of remembrance at the old age. It could be hard times one passed through, a success story or an adventure. It is normal human weakness to imagine oneself in the role of a hero in such experiences. They have their value only as 'light-reading material'. That is how I want readers to look at the events portrayed in the 'Recollections' part of the book.

I take this opportunity to express my thanks to Notion Press Media Pvt Ltd for undertaking printing and publication of my book.

M B Nair 20 July, 2024

Part I

IDLE THOUGHTS

Bhagavad Geetha, as I Understand It

Vasudev Krishna's advice to Arjuna during the Battle of Kurukshetra is what is popularly known as 'Bhagavad Geetha' or 'Geethopadesh'. It is part of the epic *Mahabharata*, authorship of which is attributed to the legendary sage Veda Vyasa.

Attempts have been made to assign a historical date for the Battle of Kurukshetra, with research suggesting the tenth or the ninth century BC as the possible period. As the legend goes, contents of the epic *Mahabharata* were, for the first time, narrated by disciples of Veda Vyasa to King Janamejaya, great-grandson of Arjuna, during a ritual (*yaga*) in Janamejaya's court. Thereafter the epic gained circulation through storytellers and was transmitted from generation to generation in the oral tradition. It appeared in writing much later. As can be expected, it would have undergone considerable distortions, exaggerations and interpolations during its oral transmission stage.

From the materialist angle, the story reduces to a succession dispute between the children of two brothers and the skirmish that followed to settle it. In the form in which it has come down to posterity, it has been a thriller for most people. Apart from becoming a barometer for the standards of that bygone age, it succeeded to a great extent in portraying in a realistic manner emotions, feelings and weaknesses of people who find a place in it. For intellectuals, what matters most, from the point of its relevance, is the philosophy conveyed through it.

Background

When leaders of Kaurava and Pandava armies sounded their conch shells in the battlefield of Kurukshetra indicating their readiness to start the war, Arjuna asked Krishna to take his chariot to the middle of the two armies facing each other so that he could clearly see the people with whom he would be fighting. Krishna drove the chariot accordingly and positioned it in the middle of the two armies. Arjuna spotted his great-grandfather Bhishma, teacher Dronacharya, relatives and friends in the army facing him and became grief-stricken. His reluctance to fight with them and Krishna's efforts to dispel his doubts and goad him to perform his duties constitute what came down to us as Geethopadesh.

Krishna's advice

When Arjuna showed reluctance to fight, Krishna reminded him that he was a Kshatriya (warrior by caste) and, as a Kshatriya, it was his duty to protect cherished values (*dharma*). In the performance of duty if he had to kill someone, he should do it unhesitatingly. Any failure in this regard would amount to dereliction of duty. Moreover, if he refused to fight, he would lose respect as a Kshatriya, and dishonour was worse than death. In the battle, he might get killed in which case he would attain martyrdom or conquer and enjoy an earthly kingdom. He should maintain steadiness and be prepared to accept success and failure with equanimity. Whether to perform prescribed duty or not was for him to decide. In either case, there would be a result over which he would have no control. Better to perform duty and face the result than run away from it. If he was fighting as part of his prescribed duty without bothering about loss or gain, victory or defeat, he would not be committing any sin. Saying this, Krishna asked him to overcome his weakness, stand up and fight.

A piece of sound advice as valid today as it would have been three thousand years back. A soldier should not be weighed down by any consideration other than his sense of duty as a soldier. Sentiments or emotions should not override his sense of judgement.

Strictly speaking, Geetopadesh should have ended here. But it went on to become a discourse in the form of Arjuna's doubts and Krishna's clarifications lasting for three or four hours. Indeed, it became an exposition of the essence of the *Vedas*. To be kept waiting for such a long time with a philosophical discourse like this would be a demoralising experience for an army in battle-readiness. That compels us to think that most of what came down to us as Geetopadesh could be later additions, particularly during the oral transmission stage of the epic.

Arjuna's worry was about killing his relatives and friends, particularly his great-grandfather Bhishma and his teacher Dronacharya. He felt that a victory at the cost of the lives of these people who were worthy of worship would be meaningless. Everything he would enjoy after this victory would be tainted with their blood. For this, Krishna's answer was that the material body was bound to perish one day or the other, and the embodied soul could neither kill nor be slain. It would manifest again as life in another material body. A sober person was not bewildered by this change. Their death should, therefore, be no cause for worry for a learned person like Arjuna.

This answer might have looked alright at that time, but today, it may look somewhat strange. While killing an enemy in battle may be justified on the grounds of expediency, a philosophical speculation (transmigration of soul) cannot be used to belittle a crime. In any case, a person charged with murder under the prevailing legal systems cannot expect acquittal on this ground.

The Supernatural in Bhagavad Geetha

In Texts 1 to 3, Chapter 4 of Bhagavad Geetha, Vasudev Krishna tells Arjuna that he was repeating what God revealed to mankind long ago. This revelation included the concept of a Supreme God.

As can be seen from the early part of *Rig Veda*, Aryans during their migrant stage were polytheists. As they moved on to the settled agricultural stage, *Sanatanadharma* (Hinduism) with its monotheism evolved. By the time of Kurukshetra Battle, the concept of a Supreme God as the be-all and end-all of the universe seems to have become well established as part of the Aryan faith.

In Chapter 9, we find an elaboration of this concept. The Supreme God pervades the entire universe and is the source of all creations. The cosmic order manifests and unmanifests under the will of this Supreme God. He is the Absolute Truth and the Ultimate Knowledge; He is life in all living beings. Ignorance and false ego prevent human beings from understanding God. A person who overcomes these weaknesses and attains true knowledge will realise that God is all-pervasive and that each living being is part of this Supreme God (*Aham brahmmasmi* or *Tattwamasi*).

The Supreme God is concerned with the well-being of all living entities. As mentioned in Text 10 of Chapter 3, He created them along with everything desirable for living happily. He created the fourfold division in human society (*varna dharma*), as stated in Text 13 of Chapter 4, taking into consideration the natural dispositions of human beings (*sathwa guna, rajo guna and tamo guna*) for the smooth functioning of society. Whenever moral and ethical standards deteriorate in society, He manifests Himself and intervenes for the deliverance of those following the righteous path, annihilation of those gone astray and re-establishment of just order (*dharmasamstha*) as pointed out in Texts 7 and 8 of Chapter 4.

In Bhagavad Geetha, as it has come down to us, Vasudev Krishna is portrayed as this Supreme God. He is said to have shown his real form to Arjuna after giving him divine vision (Texts 5 and 8, Chapter 11).

According to Ruchika Sharma (article dated 24 August 2016, Scroll.in), the first mention of Vasudev Krishna appears as early as the sixth century BC in the *Chandogya Upanishad*. He is shown as the son of Devaki (*Devaki Puthra*). Panini's *Ashtopadhyayi* (fourth century BC) presents a deified Krishna and gives details about the tribe to which he originally belonged – the Vrishnis (Krishna acquired the name 'Varshneya' from this connection). *Indicca*, the document left by Megasthenes (Greek Ambassador to Mourya Court) dated to the third century BC, speaks about the Surasenas, a branch of the Yadva-Vrishni tribe, worshipping Krishna in Mathura. These evidences point out that by about the fourth century BC (about five hundred years after the Battle of Kurukshetra) only, Krishna got deified and began to be worshipped as an incarnation of God. In *Bhagavatha Purana*, dated to the sixth century AD, Krishna assumes the form of the Supreme God.

Original *Mahabharata* does not mention Krishna's childhood days. It depicts him as a mature man respected by friends and foes alike for his wisdom and statesmanship. Pandavas leaned heavily on him for his advice during the Battle of Kurukshetra. It is in *Harivamsa* (fourth century AD), a later appendage to the original epic, that Krishna's childhood days appear. There also he appears only as a normal person born to Vasudeva of the Yadava clan and Devaki, daughter of Mathura chieftain Ugrasena. His early days were spent as a cowherd boy (*Gopala bala*) in Nandagaon village. After he moved to Mathura, he had his education under Sage Sandipani. His amorous life and dalliance with milkmaids (*gopikas*) forming events of his younger days are legends woven and added to the Krishna story after the Yadava-Vrishni clan began to mingle with the nomadic Ahir tribe, which was still at the promiscuous male-female relationship stage in its social evolution.

There is another view on this point, as brought out by Suvira Jaiswal in her book *The Origin and Development of Vaishnavism*. The priestly class of Aryan society facing the onslaught of Buddhism and Jainism caught hold of the devotional cult growing around Vasudev Krishna to re-establish its authority. That is how Vasudev Krishna, a cowherd boy, became the friend and adviser to Pandavas and, finally, the Supreme God. His advice to Arjuna and the exposition of *Sanatanadharma* in Bhagavad Geetha would become God's revelations thereby becoming eligible to claim sanctity.

These findings would lead us to the conclusion that the legendary Vasudev Krishna became noticeable for his wisdom and statesmanship in the epic *Mahabharata,* and human ingenuity and fantasising ability injected divinity into him in course of time.

Cycle of birth and death, salvation

In Texts 12 and 13 of Chapter 2, Krishna tells Arjuna: 'Never was there a time when I did not exist or you or all these kings; nor in future shall any of us cease to exist. The embodied soul passes through childhood, youth, and old age in this body and enters another body upon death'. In Texts 16 to 18 of Chapter 2, he says: 'By studying the nature of the soul and the body, philosophers have concluded that while the body is subject to change, the soul remains unchanged; while the body is perishable, the soul is indestructible, immeasurable, invisible and eternal'.

Rebirth of living beings is a concept that developed exclusively in the Indian philosophical system. Hinduism believes in an indestructible, imperishable soul residing in the perishable body and manifesting again as life in another body when the existing body perishes. Jainism and Buddhism believe life as a continuous process thereby accepting the concept of rebirth. Sikhism also subscribes to the concept of rebirth, and considers it an aspect of life determined by one's deeds. Rebirth can be in any form – an animal or a plant. According to Gautama Buddha, good deeds in this life elevate life on rebirth while bad deeds degrade it.

Each of these religions lays down its own method for liberation from the cycle of birth and death. Hinduism believes in breaking this cycle and becoming one with the Supreme through *jnana yoga, dhyana yoga, karma yoga,* or *bhakti yoga.* For Jainism, the suggested method is asceticism and meditation. Buddhism believes in following the eightfold path laid down by Gautama

Buddha as the way to end rebirth. For Sikhism, leading a simple and pious life is the way for liberation from the cycle of birth and death and merger with the *Akal.* According to Jainism, life in human form is the opportunity to work for liberation from the cycle of birth and death.

Why should one think of liberation from the cycle of birth and death? What harm is there if existing life is followed by many more lives?

The aim of liberation from the cycle of birth and death as stated in Text 51 of Chapter 2 is to escape from miserable existence in this world. Life is full of miseries and troubles, manmade or caused by nature. Instead of a repeat of this miserable existence through rebirths, is it not better to break the cycle with the existing life? That is what the ancient Indian philosophical system asked.

A critical examination of the concept of rebirth and liberation from the cycle of birth and death will tempt us to believe that philosophical thinking of the age was apparently caught in a Catch-22 situation when it brought out the idea of an indestructible, imperishable soul distinct from the perishable body. A question that would naturally arise in this context would be where this soul would go when the body perished. It was to provide an answer to this question that the idea of rebirth came in. But then, continuation of miserable existence came in as an irritant. As an answer to this problem, ways to break the cycle of birth and death and reach the stage of eternal happiness had to be brought in.

If life is considered a part of the universal energy, as held in modern rational thinking, and if that energy is considered as going back and merging with the universal pool on the death of the living being, the idea of rebirth will lose its relevance.

A word about the miserable existence pointed out by the philosophers.

According to Texts 62 to 65 of Chapter 2, thoughts about material pleasures lead to attachment towards objects of the senses and from that attachment develops lust (*kama*). From lust arises anger (*krodha*). From anger arises delusion (*moha*), and from delusion arises bewilderment of memory (*smritivibhrama*). At that stage, one loses one's intelligence (*buddhi*) and falls down into the material world of miseries. For one who can control one's senses and detach oneself from desire for material pleasures and sense objects, the world of miseries will cease to exist.

Gautama Buddha's thoughts were also on similar lines. According to him, *dukkha* (sorrow, unhappiness, suffering, anxiety, or dissatisfaction) arises from ignorance (*avidya*). All living beings longed for happiness and directed their efforts towards that objective. However, the incorrect notion that material gains or sensual pleasures would bring happiness led them to greater unhappiness. The eightfold path suggested by him was the way to get out of this miserable existence.

For the Jain faith, the soul, which is otherwise pure, gets defiled by bad deeds and that defiled soul causes unhappiness for living beings. Through asceticism and meditation, the soul can be cleansed of such defilement and such a cleansed soul will enjoy eternal happiness.

Living a simple and pious life is the suggested remedy in the Sikh faith.

Even if we discard the notion of the cycle of birth and death and liberation, the method suggested for eliminating or reducing miseries in life appears to have some validity. It is common knowledge that a simple and contented life can bring greater mental peace and happiness than wealth or power can.

But this is only one aspect of miseries in life. Miseries can be caused not only by desire for material comforts but also by various other factors like old age, incurable diseases, natural calamities, exploitation by fellow beings etc. Renunciation or detachment alone cannot solve miseries arising out of these factors. While manmade problems should look for manmade solutions without expecting intervention by imagined supernatural powers, problems caused by natural forces beyond the control of living beings will have to be faced squarely. To the extent it is possible for living beings to solve them using powers bestowed on them by nature, they have to use these powers and come out successfully. What lies beyond that has to be endured as realities or facts of life.

Happiness and unhappiness are relative terms, and one can be visualised only as a contrast to the other. Eternal or perpetual happiness can only be a figment of imagination.

Duty without desire for results (Nishkama Karma)

When Arjuna sat down in the chariot showing his reluctance to fight, Krishna reminded him of his duty as a Kshatriya and asked him to stand up and fight. Arjuna then pleaded with Krishna not to compel him to fight, pointing out the consequences of war (Texts 31 to 44, Chapter 1). Krishna had, therefore, to go into greater detail on duty and its consequences to convince Arjuna that his worries were misplaced.

Everyone is forced to act helplessly in life according to one's acquired nature (*guna*). No one can avoid work even for a moment (Text 5, Chapter 3). Non-performance of work will affect even continuity of life (Text 8, Chapter 3). To perform or not to perform a prescribed duty is left to a person. In either case, there will be a result over which that person will have no control (Text 47, Chapter 2).

Work creates bondage (*karma bandham*). If work is for sense gratification, it creates desire or attachment (*kama*), and desire generates anger (*krodha*). Anger is responsible for delusion (*lobha*) and delusion for bewilderment (*moha*). In that state of bewilderment, a person loses peace of mind (Text 63, Chapter 2). Without peace of mind, there can be no happiness (Text 66, Chapter 2).

He who is satisfied with whatever gain comes of its own accord and who is steady in success and failure never gets entangled in work (Text 22, Chapter 4). A person whose endeavours are without desire for sense gratification is free from bondage. A person engaged in normal activities is free from sinful reactions of work if those activities are without attachment to results. (Texts 19 to 24, Chapter 4).

One should not consider oneself the cause or the result of one's action (Text 47, Chapter 2).

Pandavas considered their claim in the succession dispute just, and decided to fight for it after all efforts to settle the dispute peacefully failed. Once that decision was taken, it was incorrect on the part of Arjuna to back out. He should not worry about the consequences because he was not the cause for them. As long as he was fighting for a just cause without any selfish motive, no bondage or sinful reaction would come upon him.

This, in essence, is the philosophy of duty without desire for results (*nishkama karma*) propounded in the Bhagavad Geetha. In fact, this is the central message of Geetopadesh.

Nishkama karma, opposite of *sakama karma* or selfish action, has been variously explained as 'duty for duty's sake' or 'detached involvement'. It is neither a negative attitude nor indifference, and has found many advocates in modern business circles where the emphasis has shifted to ethical business practices adhering to intrinsic human values. While *sakama karma* looks at job satisfaction through external rewards and can lead to unethical practices in workplace, *nishkama karma* turns work into a pursuit of excellence.

The concept of *nishkama karma* has been a topic for debate among scholars. According to Swami Vivekananda, a *nishkama karrmi* is one who is actively involved in worldly duties, but this involvement is without any selfish motive. For Aurobindo, *nishkama karma* meant desirelessness, i.e., duty without good or bad desires.

Seeing Kaurava army in all readiness to start the war, Arjuna tells Krishna: 'limbs of my body are quivering, my face is drying up, my whole body is trembling, my hair is standing on its end, my bow is slipping from my hand and my skin is burning. I am unable to stand, I am forgetting myself, my mind is reeling (Texts 28 to 30, Chapter 1)'. What does this imply? Did Arjuna lose his self-confidence when he saw the enemy force in battle-formation? Or was it the thought about the consequences of war (narrated by him in Texts 31 to 45 of Chapter 1) that pushed him into this shape? And then he tells Krishna: 'I am confused about my duty and have lost my composure. I am approaching you as a disciple. Please instruct me what course I should adopt (Text 7, Chapter 2)'.

What made him a confused man seeking advice from Krishna as to what he should do? Was it again his lack of self-confidence or the thought about the consequences of war? This was the question that attracted attention.

Arjuna was a Kshatriya trained in warfare from childhood days. He became the favourite student of his teacher, Dronacharya, because of his excellence during training. After his training, he was acknowledged as the topmost archer of his time (*sarvasreshta dhanurdhar*). And the Battle of Kurukshetra was not his first battle exposure. He had gone through it earlier, at least twice -- first, when Pandavas without an army met Panchal Naresh Drupad in the battlefield, and next, when he, along with Prince Uttar, handled the Kaurava force when the latter invaded Virat territory. On both occasions, he had shown unusual bravery and presence of mind. On the eve of the Battle of Kurukshetra, he even took an oath not to use his superior weapons because using them would make it an unequal battle and, therefore, unfair. Known facts being so, it is rather difficult to think that such a person would lose self-confidence at the sight of an enemy force in battle-formation.

With all that, one should give a small allowance for what is known as human weakness. Recorded incidents indicate that even experienced generals were not free from it. Napoleon Bonaparte corrected a young officer under him who was confident of victory in the Battle of Waterloo, saying that the officer was right the day before. Arthur Wellesley (Duke of Wellington) was seen lying down under a tree with a paper over his face before the battle began. They were uncertain about the outcome of the battle, and their behaviour became somewhat erratic as the countdown for the battle started. Krishna's first reaction to Arjuna's reluctance to fight is indicative of this point.

He asks Arjuna: 'How has this weakness come upon you at this hour of crisis? (Text 2, Chapter 2)'.

Perhaps, 'Consequences of war' were brought in as a cover-up for this 'weakness'. Let us keep aside 'lack of self-confidence' because of its improbability, and examine the 'consequences of war' postulate. Arjuna's greatest worry was killing so many relatives and friends, particularly his respected great-grandfather Bhishma and teacher Dronacharya. A victory at the cost of their lives had no value for him, and he felt that everything he would possess after such a victory would be tainted with their blood. Another worry was the sin he would be committing by destroying family and society.

Amartya Sen takes note of Arjuna's sensitivity to consequences of action and feels that it is an important factor in decision-making (Amartya Sen – *The idea of justice*). What happens to the world must matter and be significant in our moral and political thinking, particularly the significance of human lives.

But then, was Arjuna really looking at the well-being of society at large? He seems to be concerned with the killing of his kinsmen and friends only. He had no word for the 'unknown soldiers' who, in large numbers, would be laying down their lives for Pandavas and Kauravas during the battle. What is more, he seems to be concerned more with the sin coming upon him than the agonies of people being killed. These arguments take away the sheen from the 'consequences of war' postulate projected in the debate.

Sen also appreciates Arjuna's decision to seek guidance from Krishna for taking a proper decision. That underlines the importance of incorporating an impartial spectator into the decision-making process. The decision one takes may be flawed, particularly when confronted with conflicting thoughts. In such a circumstance, it is better to depend on a person who is considered capable of providing correct guidance.

A point that arises here is Krishna's impartiality. No doubt, he declared neutrality in the dispute between Pandavas and Kauravas right from the beginning and announced his decision not to take up arms for either side. While accepting Arjuna's request to be his charioteer (*sarathi*), he gave his army to Kauravas at Duryodhana's request. But his advice to Pandavas during the war would give an impression that he was interested in their victory for whatever reason he had, and he was ready to condone even unfair practices on their part for winning the war. The question, therefore, is whether Arjuna was looking for an 'impartial spectator' who would guide him on to the righteous path or merely a friend who would help him to come out of the confused state in which he found himself.

Sen considers Krishna a person who puts more stress on duty-based reasoning than on the consequence of action when deciding a course of action. Krishna wanted Arjuna to do his duty without bothering about the consequences of his action. As a warrior and a general on whom his side relied, Arjuna had an obligation to fight and he could not run away from it. Pushed to its extreme, this would mean that one should not back out from one's obligations even if the whole world is going to be destroyed while fulfilling them. Can one totally ignore the consequence of one's action, particularly when the issue is of national or international importance?

A closer look at Mahabharatha would reveal that Krishna was not unconcerned with the consequences of war. It was to avert the tragic consequences of war that he undertook the role of an arbitrator in the dispute. What he told Arjuna was that non-performance of duty also would have a consequence (Text 47, Chapter 2) and, therefore, he should not worry about consequences. Arjuna's non-involvement would, in all probability, lead to the defeat of Pandavas, in which case a greater calamity for family and society could be expected from the victorious Kauravas, and Arjuna would have to face it helplessly because he would have no control over it.

Krishna had, on one occasion, bluntly told Pandavas that he was on their side not merely because they were his cousins but because he felt that their claim in the succession dispute was just. So Pandavas were, according to Krishna, fighting for a righteous cause. Opting out of or not getting involved in such a war amounts to tacitly condoning injustice. So Arjuna had no choice but to fight.

As regards Arjuna's fear of committing a sin through his action and its consequences, Krishna's rejoinder was that if one was carrying out one's prescribed duties without any attachment to results, one would not be affected by sinful reactions of work (Text 21, Chapter 4).

Standard dictionary meaning of the word 'sin' is transgression of moral or religious law. Prescribed duties are divinely ordained. God created the caste system (*chaturvarnyam*), taking into consideration the natural disposition of people (*guna*) and assigning duties to each caste (Text 13, Chapter 4). Performance of prescribed duties, therefore, could never be a transgression of moral or religious law. Only duty performed with selfish motive would produce sinful reactions, according to Krishna.

This idea finds a place in modern jurisprudence. Action of a person committing murder is a punishable offence, whereas the judge pronouncing death sentence on the criminal is free from guilt, motive being the deciding factor in each case. One becomes a culpable homicide while the other a just punishment.

A point to be highlighted here is that the term 'nishkama' (desireless) is in the context of one's prescribed duty only, and it has a social significance. Complete detachment and renunciation (*vairagya*) are advocated only in the context of self-realisation and merger with the Supreme by an individual. *Sanatanadharma* does not advocate suppression of desires arising out of basic instincts like hunger and sex. On the other hand, it believes in the fullness of life. The *ashramadharma* concept makes it clear.

The metaphysical in Bhagavad Geetha

As Bal Gangadhar Tilak points out in his *Srimad Bhagavad Gita Rahasya*, if Arjuna were to seek guidance from a materialist, the latter would have critically considered the palpable profit or loss of it to Arjuna personally as also the results of it on society as a whole and would have decided whether the fight was just or unjust, because materialists do not accept any other test for determining the goodness or badness of a particular action. But such an answer would not have satisfied Arjuna. What he wanted to know was whether his action would be moral (*dharma*) or immoral (*adharma*) from the metaphysical point of view. Krishna had, therefore, to go into metaphysical issues like self-realisation and transcendental knowledge to remove Arjuna's doubts.

Self-realisation

Who am I? Only the material body felt through sense perception? Or is there anything more than that? Philosophers of ancient Aryan society pondered over this question and came up with the concept of the invisible soul (*atman*) residing in the visible living body (*deha*).

Self-realisation implies understanding of this invisible soul. Any effort in self-realisation needs concentration, that is, focusing thought on the issue. And there can be no concentration unless distracting factors like attachment to material objects, desire for sense gratification, ego etc are eliminated. Successfully conquering them by controlling senses and proceeding on intuitive lines, a person reaches the stage of divine consciousness and at that stage it would be possible to experience things which remained hidden earlier.

As Krishna tells Arjuna (Text 60, Chapter 2), senses are so strong and impetuous that they can carry away the mind of even a man of discrimination. If the effort to control the senses fails, there is no chance of reaching the stage of divine consciousness or remaining there even after reaching it.

Anyone who wishes to experience the state of divine consciousness through the intuitive method should take advice from a spiritual master who is capable of imparting knowledge (Text 34, Chapter 4).

Situated in divine consciousness, one sees one's soul (*jeevatma*) as part of the universal soul (*paramatma*). That vision helps one to feel the oneness in all living beings. What is more, in that state, one does not find any distinction between happiness and unhappiness, friendship and enmity, love and hatred; one is not affected by emotions and feelings that affect ordinary people.

A self-realised person has no duty to perform, nor has he any reason for not performing duty (Texts 17 and 18, Chapter 3). Kings like Janaka continued to perform duty even after their self-realisation to set an example to others (Text 20, Chapter 3).

Transcendental Knowledge

Transcendental knowledge is a synonym for experiencing the Supreme God. Acquiring this knowledge is considered as the aim of all spiritual exercises.

With the advancement from polytheism to monotheism, the supernatural of the early stage assumed the form of a Supreme God in Aryan society. Ever since this idea evolved, philosophers have been engaged in defining the attributes of this Supreme God and making Him as real as possible to ordinary people. Experiencing this Supreme God, considered a possibility, and merging with Him would 'liberate' human beings from their miserable existence in this world.

Philosophers of early Aryan society suggested various methods for attainment of this transcendental knowledge, and these methods go under the collective name *yoga*.

Yoga

What does *yoga* mean? In Text 48 of Chapter 2, Krishna tells Arjuna: *'Samatuam yoga uchyate'*, and in Text 50 of the same chapter, he says: *'Yoga karmasu kaushalam'*. Bal Gangadhar Tilak, in his *Gita Rahasya,* interprets the term in Text 48 as 'equability' and that in Text 50 as 'skill in action'. If we take the context in which Krishna used these two terms, we may say *yoga* in Text 48 is 'equability in success and failure', and in Text 50, it is 'skilful management between good and evil'. So our duty (*karma*), knowledge (*jnanam*), devotion (*bhakti*) or meditation (*dhyanam*) becomes *yoga* when we go about it in a systematic and disciplined manner without being influenced by extraneous factors like success and failure, good and evil, etc. The aim of *yoga*, as already stated, is the attainment of transcendental knowledge.

Karma yoga

Action originating from material consciousness of the living being is *karma*, as Krishna tells Arjuna (Text 3, Chapter 8). We are all engaged in *karma* always. We breathe, and that is *karma*; we speak, and that is *karma*; we listen, and that is *karma*; we eat, and that is *karma*. As Krishna tells Arjuna: 'everyone is forced to act helplessly according to one's natural disposition (*guna*); no one can remain inactive even for a moment' (Text 5, Chapter 3).

Karma, for our consideration, generally falls into two categories. One, as an individual carrying out responsibilities as a student, a householder or as an old person, and two, as a member of society carrying out assigned social responsibilities. Work in the first case is for advancement of self and in the second case, for the well-being of society.

Arjuna could not decide whether he should conquer or allow to be conquered and asked Krishna which was better for him (Texts 6 and 7, Chapter 2). Obviously, this question was from a moral point of view. This brings in the notion of a morally justifiable or unjustifiable action. Obeying his father's command, Parasurama killed his mother Renuka; to keep up his father's promise to Kaikeyi, Ramachandra accepted self-imposed exile (*vanavas*); Bhishma vowed celibacy to fulfil his father's desire to get Satyavati as his spouse. At the same time, we have the instance of Prahlada worshipping Vishnu, disobeying his father's command. Scholars applied their mind to this issue and came to the conclusion that morality or immorality of an action would depend on the time, place, and purpose. What is more, a means by itself can neither be moral nor immoral; it is the end to which it is directed that determines its character. Krishna's answer to Arjuna and his approval of the apparently questionable methods used for the elimination of Bhishma, Drona and Karna during the battle are indicative of this line of thinking.

To fight, or not to fight? That was the question before Arjuna. If he fought, his action would lead to loss of life for many, including his respected great-grandfather Bhishma and teacher Dronacharya, and if he refused to fight, he would betray people who placed their faith in him. It was a difficult choice. But we should know that this was not something peculiar to Arjuna alone; everyone, big or small, would have gone through such a situation some time or the other in one's life. Legends and chronicles are replete with stories representing this theme. Shakespeare's *Coriolanus* is an example. His hero, Caius Marcius, faced a similar problem -- sack Rome and look for the dead bodies of his mother and wife in the debris or back out from the deal struck with Tullus Aufidius to invade Rome and face the consequence. In such a situation, a person may seek advice from a trusted friend, but in the end, it is up to that person to decide which way to go. As Krishna tells Arjuna, whichever way he chooses, there will be a consequence over which he will have no control (Text 47, Chapter 2).

To a question from Arjuna what impelled a person to commit a sinful act, Krishna's answer was that it was desire (*kama*) and anger (*krodha*) born out of the mode of passion (*rajoguna*) (Texts 36 and 37, Chapter 3). They lead a person to delusion (*lobha*) and bewilderment (*moha*). A person who is overpowered by desire and anger loses control over his senses. Sinful acts originate from uncontrolled senses. To avoid sinful acts, desire and anger, the symbols of sin should be curbed by regulating the senses (Text 41, Chapter 3).

As Swamy Vivekananda says, 'There cannot be work without motive' (*The Complete Works of Swamy Vivekananda, Vol 1*). Some people want money, some want fame and some want power. And their motives guide their work. The same is the case with desire (*kama*). Can we think of any activity without desire? As Bal Gangadhar Tilak says (*Gita Rahasya*), 'If tomorrow all living beings decide to say goodbye to Lord Kama and observe celibacy the whole of their lives, the entire living creation will come to an end within fifty or at most one hundred years'. Desire is the motive force behind progress. Desire for food and sex arises from basic instincts like survival and procreation. Even a person renouncing everything and becoming a *sanyasi* is guided by the desire for salvation (*moksha*). And of anger, quoting a verse from *Mahabharatha,* Tilak says: 'He who gets angry (on account of injustice) and who does not submit (to insult) is truly a man. He who does not get angry or annoyed is neither a man nor a woman'.

One may have to go through many of what may be termed 'symbols of sin' during one's lifetime, particularly at the householder stage. There is no running away from them. Any attempt to suppress basic instincts like hunger or sex may turn counterproductive, leading to perversions and chaos. At best, one may try not to be overpowered by temptations which lead people to act in an irresponsible manner. At the old age, it would be easier to control temptations since most temptations that pester people during their youth would have disappeared at that age. The concept of *ashrama dharma* which leaves renunciation and spiritual journey to the last phase of life was brought in later, presumably, taking into consideration the difficulty of following the advice during earlier stages.

Work for work's sake. Do not allow yourself to be overpowered by distractions like ego, desire, and anger. You should not bother about success and failure or the consequence of your action. Such an approach alone can give you peace of mind and happiness. You have to get established in that state before you begin your spiritual journey. That was the advice Krishna gave to Arjuna, and that forms the basis of *karma yoga.*

The spiritual power one attains through *karma yoga* is illustrated by the popular story of the *sanyasi* and the *karma yogi.* A person did penance for a long time to gain spiritual powers. One morning, while sitting and meditating under a tree, a bird drop fell on him. Looking up, he found that a crow sitting on a branch above was responsible for it. His angry look was sufficient to burn the crow and bring it down. He was surprised and felt that he had attained tremendous spiritual powers. With that feeling he moved out expecting venerable treatment from everyone he met. When he went to a house and announced his arrival, no one came out to receive him. He was angry. When, at last, the lady of the house turned up, the sanyasi looked at her angrily to punish her for the ill-treatment meted out to him. The lady made out his intention from his looks and told him that his trick with the crow would not work with her because what he achieved through his long penance she achieved through her dedicated service as a wife. The sanyasi became humble and touched her feet. What the story points out is that *karma yoga* also is a path to spirituality.

Karma yoga is thus a system of ethics through which a person can attain self-realisation and knowledge of the Supreme. As Swamy Vivekananda says (*Complete Works*, Vol 1), 'A *karma yogi* need not believe in any doctrine whatever. He may not believe even in God. Through his selfless work he can achieve what a scholar (*jnani*) or a believer (*bhakta*) can through knowledge or devotion.'

Jnana yoga

Jnana yoga implies the search for knowledge through the rational or the analytical method. This method rejects conclusions based on faith or belief and accepts only those which can be scientifically or logically established. The *Sankhya* and *Mimamsa* schools of thought represented this line of thinking. In ancient Greece, it took the shape of deductive and inductive methods developed by the philosopher Aristotle. In Bhagavad Geetha, we find the word '*Sankhya*' mentioned in connection with the analytical method.

Krishna tells Arjuna that a learned person knows that there is no great difference between analytical (*Sankhya*) and devotional (*bhakti*) methods. Both are meant to reach the same goal. Whatever one can achieve through the analytical method can be achieved through the devotional method also. The only difference is that one who goes by the devotional method reaches the goal faster (Texts 4 to 6, Chapter 5). One should follow the analytical method only if one is unable to follow the devotional method (Text 12, Chapter 12).

After his accidental encounter with 'gravity', Isaac Newton made a remark: 'I do not know what I may appear to the world, but to myself, I seem to have been only like a boy playing on the seashore and diverting myself in now and then finding a smoother pebble or a prettier shell than ordinary, while the great ocean of truth lay all undiscovered before me'. If we read this in conjunction with what Krishna said, it would mean that, let alone one lifetime, even a hundred lifetimes cannot take us anywhere near the ultimate truth if we proceed on the analytical lines. The devotional method is a shortcut according to Krishna.

This is not to belittle the analytical method or to suggest its abandonment on the ground that it is time-consuming and, therefore, not useful. In all probability, future may witness the emergence of the analytical method as the only dependable method in our search for truth. That may possibly mark the end of all other methods.

If the *Sankhya* and *Mimamsa* systems of ancient Aryans or the logical approach of ancient Greeks had advanced undisturbed, we would have perhaps seen tremendous progress in the analytical method today. But those systems virtually disappeared or took a back seat in course of time. Ideas developed by the Greeks revived during the post-Renaissance age, and they initiated the scientific revolution in Europe during the eighteenth century. The analytical method became the basis of modern rational thinking.

Success in both methods depends on the observance of certain disciplines. Faith in God is the basic requirement for the devotional method. The first requirement before proceeding with the analytical method, as laid down by the English philosopher and empiricist Francis Bacon (1561-1626), is that the enquirer must free his or her mind from false notions based on faith and belief or tendencies which distorted truth. Both disciplines need training and concentration.

Results obtained through the devotional method are difficult to communicate and should, for that reason, remain as individual experiences. Findings through the analytical method undergo various tests before they are considered as acceptable propositions, and the established idea should be capable of being demonstrated physically or rationally anytime, anywhere.

For the analytical method, the material world which can be perceived or understood through the senses alone is reality, whereas for the devotional method, the material world is only an illusion, and the ultimate truth lies beyond that. Layers of ignorance surrounding the inner self prevent a person from experiencing it. 'Who am I?' 'What for am I here?' etc are questions for which the analytical method has no answer. It does not seem to bother about them also since its primary aim is to explain what is seen as natural phenomena in rational terms rather than trying to find out their root cause which may be unknowable. This method takes life to be part of the invisible universal energy. It goes back and merges with the universal pool on the death of a living being.

The classical *Sankhya* system denies the existence of God on metaphysical grounds. *Sankhya* theorists of ancient days argued that an unchanging God could not be the source of an ever-changing world, and God was only a necessary metaphysical assumption demanded by circumstances. Bhagavad Geetha disagrees with this contention and asserts the existence of a Supreme God.

An important proposition in the *Sankhya* system is that *shunya* (nothing) can produce only *shunya*. This idea finds a place in Bhagavad Geetha too ('*Nasato vidyate bhavo*' --Text 15, Chapter 2). This proposition implies a continuity in whatever we can physically perceive through the senses, may be in different forms as a result of changes in the original. The 'Big Bang' model and the evolution theory can be related to this concept. It is this concept that prompted the analytical method to question the existence of God because a creator and creation (from nothing) cannot fit in with this concept.

Bhakti yoga

Bhakti yoga is one of the methods advocated in Bhagavad Geetha for experiencing the Supreme. It consists of concentrating one's mind, emotions, and senses on the Supreme Being.

Ever since human beings distinguished themselves from other animal species with their superior intelligence and reasoning power, a feeling that some invisible supernatural power influenced their lives and activities began to dominate their thinking. This power was given a name in their dialects (each equivalent to 'deity' in English), and it was imagined to be residing in whatever they came across, like the Sun, Moon, stars, fire, water, wind, trees, mountains etc. Any 'displeasure' of this power would adversely affect their lives and activities. By worshipping this power and offering it things dear to the worshipers like grains, clothes etc, they felt that it could be 'kept pleased'. These ideas changed as human thinking progressed, and an all-powerful Supreme God presiding over the deities of the earlier stage appeared in course of time. The aim of worship also changed, taking a metaphysical form, replacing the earlier aim of seeking help to solve everyday problems. *Bhakti yoga has its* origin in this development.

Bhakti is supreme, true, undiluted and untainted love and attachment to the Supreme God according to *Shandilya Bhakti Sutra. Bhakti* has to be understood in this sense if a person wants to proceed on the path of devotion (*bhakti yoga*) for self-realisation and transcendental knowledge. As *Chandogya Upanishad* points out, all other rites and rituals may take one to their respective results but not to the goal of self-realisation or knowledge of the Ultimate Truth. Bhagavad Geetha endorses this idea (Texts 23 to 25, Chapter 9).

'In this world, there is nothing more sublime than transcendental knowledge', says Krishna to Arjuna (Text 38, Chapter 4). Philosophers of ancient India were finding out disciplines through which one could attain this supreme knowledge. Path of selfless duty (*karma yoga*), analytical method (*jnana yoga*), path of devotion (*bhakti yoga*) and meditation (*dhyana yoga*) were the ideal methods suggested by them in the light of their experiences. Krishna explains them to Arjuna and tells him that, of all the methods, *bhakti yoga* is the simplest and the easiest.

A person who follows the *karma yoga* path should be prepared to control senses, give up all desires for material pleasures and should not develop any attachment to work. Such disciplines may be difficult for most people. Senses are so strong and impetuous that they can carry away the mind of even a man of discrimination (Text 60, Chapter 2). *Jnana yoga* demands a high degree of intelligence, and very few people possess such intelligence. This means that a large number of people, particularly low caste people and women, who are denied opportunities like others, will never be able to follow the above two paths and will be confined to their miserable existence without any hope. *Bhakti Yoga* offers a path to such people too (Text 32, Chapter 9). 'Abandon all cherished values (*dharma*) and surrender unto me' says Krishna (Text 66, Chapter 18). That, in essence, is *bhakti yoga*, and it can be practised by anyone while leading a normal life.

As already mentioned, *bhakti yoga* involves concentration on the Supreme Being who, as conceived by philosophers, is formless (*nirakara*) and imperceptible (*avyakta*). As Krishna tells Arjuna, for those whose minds are attached to the unmanifested and imperceptible feature of the Supreme God, advancement is troublesome (Text 5, Chapter 12). Human mind 'cannot understand on what to concentrate unless it has before itself, by way of support, some steady object which is perceptible to the organs' says Bal Gangadhar Tilak in his *Gita Rahasya*. For this reason, presumably, the *Upanishads* prescribed a visible form of God to represent the formless God. In some *Upanishads*, worship of the perceptible form of God in the shape of human beings is mentioned. This does not prohibit representation in other forms. Since God exists in all objects, both animate and inanimate, one can imagine His shape in any form. Form is immaterial, and what matters is the spiritual value which one assigns to it. Concentration becomes easier if the imagined form is transformed into a visible idol.

Concentration will be relevant only if we are sure that the object of concentration exists. Existence of God cannot be established through the logical or analytical method. As the *Vedic* instruction goes, '*achintya khalu ye bhava na thams tarkena yo jayet*' (do not apply logic in matters inconceivable by you). This leads us to the conclusion that faith is the only means available to us to make God a reality. That is the starting point for one who proceeds on the path of devotion (*bhakti yoga*). As Krishna tells Arjuna, 'the greatest of all *yogis* is the *yogi* who places his 'faith' in me (Text 47, Chapter 6)'.

Faith is a mental faculty which helps a person to accept a proposition which comes out of own experiences or what is heard from others. And this faculty is independent of reason or logic. There are hundreds of people who carry on their activities relying on the statements of others. Differences of opinion can arise among people, and it is for the person who wants to choose a particular opinion for guidance to decide which among the different opinions is more reliable or dependable.

It should be noted that the term faith used here is in the context of *bhakti Yoga* and is meant as a means for concentrating on the Supreme God, whose existence cannot be established through other means. In other words, it should not be a cover for any odd obscurantist idea or belief, as the consequences can be catastrophic. For example, according to Bhagavad Geeta, the caste system was created by God (Text 13, Chapter 4), and it was meant for the smooth functioning of society, taking into consideration the natural dispositions of people (*gunas*). We are not sure whether this was Krishna's observation or whether a later addition to sanctify the caste system. Historically, the caste system evolved in early Aryan society after the Aryans moved to the settled agricultural stage from their earlier migrant stage. Using this verse as a cover, high castes began to exploit lower castes in course of time, and people of lower castes were made to accept their lot meekly in the name of faith.

Faith is a means to imagine the existence of God. Having fixed up the idea of God through faith, one has to follow it up through *bhakti* (intense love for God as defined in *Shandilya Bhakti Sutra*) for self-realisation and attainment of true knowledge. This involves worship of God (*upasana*) all the time, and worship should be purposeless (*nirhetuka*), that is, it should be only for concentrating on God and not for any other purpose.

'I am the father of this universe, the mother, the support and the grandsire. I am the object of knowledge, the purifier and the syllable '*Om.*' I am also the *Rig, Saama* and *Yajur Veda*' says Krishna to Arjuna (Text 17, Chapter 9) and 'one can understand me as I am only through the devotional path' (Text 55, Chapter 18). A *bhakti yogi* who understands God through the devotional path reaches the same goal which other *yogis* reach through their respective methods.

Dhyana yoga

Meditation (*dhyana yoga*) is another path for linking oneself with the Supreme. The word *dhyanam* is derived from the Sanskrit word *dhi* which means to contemplate, reflect, think, or be occupied in thought. According to Sage Patanjali, *dhyanam* is 'incessant flow of attention on the concentrated object (*tatra prathyaikatanata dhyanam*)', and according to the *Sankhya* School of Philosophy, 'liberation of mind from all disturbing or distracting emotions, thoughts and desires (*dhyanam nirvishayam manah*)'. *Dhyanam* starts with *dharana*, i.e., concentration. Mind becomes steady and single-pointed through concentration, and when concentration leads to uninterrupted flow of thought towards one object, that becomes *dhyanam*.

No concentration (*dharana*) is possible without controlling senses. As Krishna tells Arjuna, senses are so strong and impetuous that they can forcibly carry away the mind even of a strong-minded person who makes an effort to control them (Text 60, Chapter 2). When Arjuna expressed his difficulty in controlling his senses (Text 34, Chapter 6), Krishna's reply was that, although it was difficult, it was still possible through constant practice (Text 35, Chapter 6).

Those who wish to practice *dhyana yoga* must observe certain disciplines. As Krishna tells Arjuna (Texts 1 and 2, Chapter 6), they should learn to carry out their obligatory duties without any expectation of results for their labour and start giving up desire for sense gratification (*sankalpa*). To avoid distraction, they should choose secluded places and be lonely when they engage themselves in this practice (Text 10, Chapter 6). They should regulate their food and sleep, neither too much nor too little (Text 16, Chapter 6). Only those who observe these disciplines strictly will be able to control their senses and keep their mind steady for concentration. Guidance of an experienced teacher is a must to ensure adherence to the correct procedure.

The above-mentioned disciplines constitute the preparatory stage for practicing the *ashtanga yoga* (forming part of Sage Patanjali's *Yoga Sutra*), also known as *raja yoga,* which leads one to self-realisation and transcendental knowledge through meditation (*dhyanam*). This *yoga*, as the name indicates, consists of eight limbs (*yama, niyama, asana, pranayama, pratyahara, dharana, dhyanam* and *samadhi*).

Yama (ethics of behaviour) consists of non-violence (*ahimsa*), truthfulness (*satya*), non-stealing (*asteya*), celibacy (*brahmacharya*) and non-possession (*aparigraha*).

Niyama (observance) consists of cleanliness (*shauchya*), contentment (*santosha*), austerity (*tapas*), self-study (*swadhyaya*) and devotion to God (I*shwara pranidhana*).

Asana, according to Sage Patanjali, is a physical posture in which one can be steady and comfortable. Later, the term was extended to cover different postures with different names such as *sarvangasana, bhujangasana, shirasasana, shavasana* etc in *hata yoga* and in *yoga* as a form of physical exercise.

Pranayama is the process by which life (*prana*) and mind (*manah*) are controlled by regulation of external breath.

Pratyahara means withdrawal of senses. For Patanjali, *pratyahara* is the bridge between the external (*yama, niyama, asana* and *pranayama*) and the internal (*dharana, dhyanam and samadhi*) aspects of the *yoga* system.

Dharana may be translated as 'concentration'. Senses withdrawn under *pratyahara* are further refined in this method to make them *ekagra chitta* (single-pointed concentration).

Dhyanam means contemplation or meditation. *Yoga Sutra* defines *dhyanam* as 'continuous flow of the same thought or image of the object of meditation without being distracted by any other thought'. For example, while one sees colour and brightness of the Sun at the *dharana* stage, at the *dhyanam* stage, it is only the Sun and nothing else.

Samadhi, the last limb of *ashtanga yoga,* is the state of meditative consciousness or unification of the mind and the object.

The last three stages, namely, *dharana, dhyanam and samadhi* taken together constitute integration (*samyama*). From mastery over *samyama* comes the light of awareness and insight (*tajjayat prajnaloka*), according to Sage Patanjali. At that stage, all illusions disappear, and transcendental knowledge opens up.

From the above narrative, it will be clear that *dhyana yoga* is not an easy one for an ordinary person. Even if one starts with great enthusiasm, initial enthusiasm will start waning as the discipline becomes more and more rigorous. Very few people can reach the goal successfully. What will happen to a person who gives up halfway? This was Arjuna's question to Krishna. Will such a person perish like a riven cloud with no place anywhere (Text 38, Chapter 6)? For this, Krishna's answer was that auspicious activities of a person do not meet with destruction; no evil can befall good work (Text 40, Chapter 6). If one tries again and again with dedication and determination, one is bound to reach the goal some time or the other (Text 45, Chapter 6).

Transcendental knowledge is the mature fruit of all mysticism, according to Bhagavad Geetha. A person who acquires this knowledge will see that all living beings are but part of the Supreme (Text 35, Chapter 4). For such a person, happiness and distress, heat and cold, honour and dishonour are all the same; pebble, stone, and gold, alike; no difference between friends and foes, the pious and the sinners; no desire or possessiveness (Texts 7 to 10, Chapter 6). Such a person rises above material existence and reaches the state of perfect peace and happiness (Text 15, Chapter 6).

After attainment of transcendental knowledge, what will one do during the remaining part of one's life? Strictly speaking, such a person has no duty to perform or purpose to fulfil, as Krishna tells Arjuna. This does not mean that such a person should avoid work and lead an easygoing life. People like Janaka (presumably the legendary Videha chieftain mentioned in *Valmiki Ramayana*), even after attaining perfection through *karma yoga,* continued to perform prescribed duties to set an example to others. Whatever action a great man performs, common men follow, and whatever example he sets, the world pursues. Performance of such duty should be for the welfare of mankind, not for any self-interest (Texts 18 to 21, Chapter 3).

Moksha (Salvation)

The *yoga* system mentioned above is the means for self-realisation and attainment of transcendental knowledge. When one reaches that stage through any of the *yogas*, what is there for one to look for? There is nothing more to know (Text 2, Chapter 7) and no purpose to fulfill (Text 18, Chapter 3). Only spend the remaining days of life performing selfless work in the service of mankind (Texts 19 and 20, Chapter 3) and wait for the day to leave this world. One who departs, keeping one's mind fixed on the Supreme, merges with the Supreme (Text 5, chapter 8). That is salvation (*moksha*), according to Bhagavad Geetha.

Moksha is a term in the ancient Indian philosophical system that represents emancipation, enlightenment, or liberation. In its religious sense (soteriological), it refers to freedom from *samsara,* the cycle of birth and death. In its philosophical sense (epistemological), it is self-realisation, self-knowledge, or freedom from ignorance. In the *Sanatana* tradition, *dharma* (virtuous, proper, moral life), *artha* (wealth, means of life), *kama* (sensuality, emotional fulfilment) and *moksha* (enlightenment or emancipation from the cycle of birth and death) constitute the goals of life (*purushartha*). Of these, *moksha* is *paramapurushartha* (the supreme goal). A person who attains moksha moves into eternal peace and happiness and does not have to be reborn.

The idea of *moksha* seems to have arisen from the desire for release from pain and suffering associated with life in this world. When transmigration of soul and rebirth became part of philosophical thinking, one assumption that naturally followed was that each new life would be a continuation of the previous life with all its pain and suffering. Instead of continuing such a life, it would be better to end it. For this, it would be necessary to break the cycle of birth and death. Merging with the Supreme through conscious effort during life in human form was the only way to break this cycle and attain eternal happiness.

A point worth mentioning here is the evolutionary nature of the concept of *moksha* in the Indian philosophical system. In the *Vedas*, the three goals of life, *dharma*, *artha* and *kama* find a mention. To this, *moksha* was added as the fourth goal during the *upanishadic* era.

The *Katha Upanishad*, dated to about 2500 BC, is among the earliest expositions of the concept of *moksha*. According to this *Upanishad*, liberation (*moksha*) comes from a life of inner purity and an alert mind led by intelligence (*buddhi*).

Some schools of thought in the Indian philosophical system were slow to accept the concept of *moksha*. For example, the *Mimamsa* School refused to accept the relevance of *moksha* till about the eighth century AD. Till then, *Mimamsa* scholars felt that heaven (*swarga*), an imagined place of happiness, was sufficient to answer the question as to what lay beyond this material world.

In its historical development, the concept of *moksha* appears in three different forms: *Vedic*, *yogic*, and *bhakti*. During the *Vedic* period, *moksha* was ritualistic. *Moksha* was assumed to result from properly conducted rituals, which included recitals of relevant verses from the *Vedas*. Knowledge was the means and rituals its application. During the *upanishadic* period, emphasis shifted to knowledge and rituals were considered irrelevant to attainment of *moksha*. This was the *yogic* method in which personal development and meditation became the path for attainment of *moksha*. As Adi Sankaracharya says, '*arthasya nischayo drishto, vichaarena hitoktita; na snaanena na daanena pranaayama shatena va* (by reflection, reasoning and instruction of teachers, truth is known; not by ablution, not by making donation nor by performing hundreds of breath-control exercises)'. *Bhakti yoga*, a later development, was the third historical path for attainment of *moksha* in which neither rituals nor meditation but pure love and devotion to God became the path.

In *Sankhya* literature, liberation (*moksha*) is commonly referred to as *kaivalya*. It is derived from the Sanskrit word *kevala*, meaning 'alone' or 'isolated'. Like other schools of thought in the Indian philosophical system, the *Sankhya* system also lays emphasis on knowledge, that is, knowledge of true self (*purusha*) as distinct from mind and body (*prakrti*). This knowledge is obtained by the removal of ignorance or incorrect ideas of self and the world through meditation. A self-realised person enjoys bliss and happiness unthinkable by others. For *Sankhya* philosophers, merger with the Supreme did not arise since God was only a metaphysical assumption for them.

Liberation and freedom attained during one's lifetime are referred to as *Jeevan Mukti* by *Sankhya, yoga* and *Vedanta* Schools. Some scholars contrast *Jeevanmukti* with *videhamukti* (*moksha* from *samsara* after death). According to them, *Jeevan Mukti* is the state that transforms the nature, attributes, and behaviour of an individual. When a person who attained *Jeevan Mukti* dies, that person attains *videhamukti* or liberation from the cycle of birth and death.

Different conceptions of *moksha* in Hinduism indicate the speculative nature of this idea as also the fantasising ability of human mind.

Overview

Bhagavad Geetha is an indicator of the advancement made by Indian philosophical system three thousand years back. This system was much ahead compared to those of other contemporary civilisations. While the idea of the supernatural was still at its developing stage in other civilisations, it had already matured and reached the refined stage of belief in an all-pervading Supreme Being in Indian philosophical thinking. After this development, Indian philosophers started probing the concepts of mind and soul. They started distinguishing the visible material life from spiritual life, which connected all living beings to the Supreme. Understanding this connection became a challenging problem for them. Differences of opinion led to the evolution of different schools of thought within the system.

Geetopadesh is basically the advice given by Vasudev Krishna to Arjuna in the battlefield of Kurukshetra. When Arjuna showed reluctance to fight with his relatives and friends, Krishna reminded him of his duty as a Kshatriya and asked him to stand up and fight. Arjuna was still wavering with his 'stricken conscience', and Krishna had to go into great details about the material and spiritual aspects of his duty to dispel his doubts and goad him to action. In the process, Geetopadesh became an exposition of the essence of the *Vedas*, the philosophical basis of *Sanatanadharma* or the Hindu way of life.

Many people look at Bhagavad Geetha as something sacred. That approach takes away our ability to critically examine it. To appreciate the philosophy conveyed through it and examine its relevance today, we have to bring it down from that sanctified pedestal and read it as an expression of human wisdom, wisdom of the age in which it was composed and perfected.

In Geethopadesh, we find great emphasis being placed on faith in the Supreme Being. Faith in God will not only help you to overcome impediments coming in your way but also to bring out the best in you. It is the firm base to fall back upon when exposed to calamities beyond the limit of human endurance. This is the advice which Bhagavad Geetha imparts. It is on expected lines because Bhagavad Geetha belonged to the age when the newly developed ideas of the all-pervading Supreme God were becoming dominant in Indian philosophical thinking. The *Sankhyas, Mimasikas* and *Charavakas* had not begun to show their presence questioning the validity of the concept of God during that period. We find the word '*sankhya*' mentioned in the Geethopadesh only to represent the analytical method in finding out the Ultimate Truth.

An imperishable soul residing in the perishable body, transmigration of soul, and cycle of birth and death, ideas that developed exclusively in the Indian philosophical system, find their endorsement in Bhagavad Geetha. Then comes life with all its sorrows and sufferings. To escape from this miserable existence, the cycle of birth and death has to be broken,and that is possible only through conscious effort during life in human form. Geetopadesh contains practical methods for breaking this cycle and reaching the stage of eternal peace and happiness.

These ideas do not go well with modern rational thinking which does not accept any proposition that cannot be rationally established as an all-time truth. In this line of thinking, God still remains in the realm of speculation. Life is only a part of the universal energy, and it goes back and merges with the universal pool on death. And that puts off the question of rebirth. Most miseries associated with life are manmade. Manmade problems should look for manmade solutions, not divine intervention. Human beings should try to solve them with the powers bestowed on them by nature to the extent possible. What lies beyond human capability will have to be accepted and endured as facts of life.

The *Karma Yoga* philosophy is what stands out as Bhagavad Geetha's greatest contribution to mankind. Selfless duty for the well-being of society is the highest ideal. Be satisfied with whatever gains your selfless performance of duty can bring for you. A simple and contented life can give greater peace of mind and happiness than what wealth and power can give. This is a valid message for all times, particularly for societies which suffer under materialist stress and strain.

Aryans had to wage wars with enemy forces both at their migrant and settled stages. War thus became an accepted part of state policy, and those who specialised in warfare came to be identified as Kshatriyas in the caste system. We can see an indirect endorsement of this fact in Bhagavad Geetha. Krishna reminds Arjuna of his 'duty as a Kshatriya'. Battle of Kurukshetra is portrayed as a *dharma yuddha* (just battle) to punish evildoers and establish righteousness in the world.

This tradition in Aryan society led to the evolution of an interesting principle relating to ends and means. A means by itself can neither be pure nor impure; it is the end to which it is directed that determines its purity and impurity. Vasudev Krishna's advice to Arjuna and the questionable methods adopted in eliminating Bhishma, Drona and Karna during the battle are illustrative of this line of thinking in the ancient

Indian philosophical system. Modern rational thinking seems to have adopted this idea.

<u>Annexure</u>

English Translation of Bhaktivedanta Swamy Prabhupada's Bhagavad Gita as It Is

(Texts 1 to 27 of Chapter 1, being introductory, left out in the translation)

Arjuna:

Krishna, Seeing my friends and relatives in such fighting spirit, my body is quivering, and my mouth is drying up. My whole body is trembling, my hair is standing on its end, my bow (*gandiva*) is slipping from my hand and my skin is burning. I am unable to stand. I am forgetting myself, and my mind is reeling. I see only misfortune ahead. I do not see how any good can come from killing one's own kinsmen in battle. I do not desire victory, kingdom or happiness. Even if they want to kill me, I do not wish to kill them. I am not going to fight with them even if I get the three worlds, let alone the earth, as a reward for my victory. Although these men, in their greed, see no fault in killing their own family members or quarrelling with friends, why should we who see the crime in such an act engage ourselves in it? With the destruction of family, traditional family relation is lost, and the disappearance of family relation leads to irreligion, immorality and disturbance in social harmony. It is better for me to die in the battlefield without resistance.

(Saying so, Arjuna discards his bow and arrows and sits down in the chariot.)

Krishna:

How has this weakness come upon you in this hour of crisis? It does not befit a person who knows the value of life. It does not elevate you but only leads you to infamy. Give up this petty weakness and get up.

Arjuna:

Krishna, how can I send arrows towards Bhishma and Drona who are worthy of my worship? It would be better to live in this world begging than living at the cost of the lives of these great men who are my superiors. If I kill them for the sake of worldly gains, everything I enjoy will be tainted with their blood. If we Pandavas kill Kauravas, we may not care to live. I am unable to drive away this grief and will not be able to get over it even if I win a prosperous kingdom. I am confused about my duty and am surrendering unto you as a disciple seeking your guidance.

Krishna:

While speaking like a learned person, you are grieving for what is not worthy of grief. Wise men lament neither for the living nor for the dead. Never was there a time when I did not exist, or you or all these kings; nor in future shall any of us cease to be. The embodied soul passes from childhood to youth and from youth to old age in this body and passes on to another body at death. A sober person is not bewildered by such a change. Philosophers have come to the conclusion that while the material body is subject to change and is bound to perish one day or the other, the soul is invisible, imperishable, indestructible and immutable.

The soul can neither kill nor be slain. Once these facts become clear, you will not grieve for the material body.

Happiness and distress, like cold and heat, are sense perceptions, and their appearance and disappearance are non-permanent. You must learn not only to tolerate them but also to be steady in both.

As a Kshatriya, your duty is to protect cherished values (*dharma*), and in the performance of this duty, if it becomes necessary to kill, you should unhesitatingly do it. If you fail to do so, you will be neglecting your duty and thereby losing respect as a Kshatriya. And you should know that dishonour is worse than death. In the battle, you get killed in which case you claim martyrdom, or you conquer and enjoy the earthly kingdom. Therefore, get up with determination and fight. If you fight for the sake of fighting without considering happiness or distress, loss or gain, victory or defeat, you are not committing any sin.

So far, I have described the knowledge attained through analytical reasoning *(Sankhya)*. Now, I shall describe work without expectation of gains (*nishkama karma*). If you act on the basis of what I say, you will be freed from the bondage of work (*karmabandham*). In this endeavour, there is no loss or diminution, and a little advancement on this path will protect you from the worst type of fear.

For a resolute person, the aim is clear; an irresolute mind strays. Most people are carried away by the flowery language of the Vedas, and they think that by performing the rituals laid down therein, they would gain wealth, power and happiness. In the pursuit of this aim, their resoluteness is lost. Rise above this ritualistic side, free yourself from all dualities and anxieties for gain and safety and be established in yourself. For a person who is so established, the essence of the *Vedas* would become clear.

Performance of duty is in your hands, not the result. You are not the cause of the result of your deeds. Never try to run away from your duty. Perform your duty without bothering about success and failure. Such an approach makes it a discipline (*yoga*). Discard abominable activities and concentrate on your duty. Only selfish people will look for results for their work. One who engages in selfless work can get rid of good and bad results of one's duty in this life itself. Therefore, engage in selfless work which is an art in itself. By doing selfless duty, great sages liberated themselves from the cycle of birth and death.

When your mind gets out of the forest of illusion, you become indifferent to what is heard and what is yet to be heard. Purify your mind by giving up your desire for material pleasures. Then, concentrate on self-realisation. You will attain the stage of transcendental consciousness (*sthithaprajna*). When you reach that stage, you will not be affected by sorrow or happiness, and you will be free from attachment, fear and anger. Even if you are in the midst of the material world, you will be unmoved by the happenings around you. As a tortoise draws its limbs into its shell, a person who attains divine consciousness can withdraw his senses from material objects. Experience of a higher state enables him to withdraw without any conscious effort.

Senses are very powerful and impetuous, and they can carry away the mind of even a man of discrimination. A person of divine consciousness in such a situation keeps his consciousness fixed in me and controls his senses.

Thoughts about worldly pleasures create attachment. From attachment develops desire (*kama*), and from desire is born anger (*krodha*). From Anger arises delusion (*lobha*), and from delusion, bewilderment (*moha*). When that happens, one loses discrimination and falls down to the material world. If you can keep yourself free from attachment and keep your senses under control, you can expect blessings from the Lord. With such blessings, you become free from miseries, and in that happy state, divine consciousness arises.

A person without divine consciousness and a steady mind cannot have peace, and without peace there can be no happiness. As a strong wind sweeps away a boat in water, even a single instance of sensory deviation can sweep away a man's divine consciousness. One whose senses are restrained alone can be steady in one's divine consciousness.

What is night for all beings is the time of awakening for the self-controlled, and the time of awakening for all beings, the sages see as beginning of night. A person not disturbed by desires and not affected by false ego alone can have peace, not the one who strives to fulfil such desires. That is the way of spiritual life. One who proceeds in that plane is not bewildered and reaches the kingdom of God at the end.

Arjuna:

Why do you want me to engage myself in such ghastly warfare if you think that a spiritual life is better than a life seeking material gains?

Krishna:

As I said earlier, self-realisation is possible through two different ways, one through philosophical speculation (*jnana yoga*) and the other through devotional service (*karma yoga*).

By abstaining from work, you cannot avoid results; nor can renunciation (*sannyasa*) alone bring perfection. With qualities acquired from nature (*guna*), each one acts helplessly. No one can remain absolutely inactive, even for a moment. One who controls senses without controlling desire for sense objects deludes oneself. A person who controls desires and begins to do selfless work is at a higher level. Performing duty is better than non-performance. Even for maintenance of health, work is necessary. Therefore, perform your prescribed duty, and it should be selfless as otherwise it causes bondage in the material world.

God created human beings along with all the necessary things required for their survival. He prescribed duties (*yajna*) also for them, the performance of which will please nature. A gratified nature will bestow upon them prosperity and happiness. These duties are prescribed in the *Vedas*, and the *Vedas* originated from God. There is, therefore, divinity in duty. Those who consume food after due performance of those duties are free from all sins.

One who attains self-realisation has no duty to perform. A self-realised person has no purpose to fulfil, nor has he any reason for not performing duty. Kings like Janaka attained self-realisation through their selfless duty. Even such persons continued to perform duty only to become an example for others. Whatever action a great man performs, common men follow. Whatever example he sets, the world pursues. Even though I have no necessity to perform any duty and have no need for anything, I do my prescribed duties. If I fail to engage myself in my prescribed duties, men will follow my path, and I will be the cause of ruining peace in this world. While an ignorant person performs duty with attachment to results, a wise man does so without attachment for the sake of leading the ignorant onto the right path. He should not discourage them from doing work because of their attachment to results. On the other hand, they should be allowed to carry on, and through advice and persuasion, he should lead them on to the right path.

Bewildered by false ego, an ignorant person thinks he is the doer of activities. Once you come to know the absolute truth, you will realise that you are only part of the universe and what is happening is what nature decides.

Surrendering all your deeds unto me, without desire for results, without claim for proprietorship, without being lethargic, carry out your duty, which at present is fighting with the enemy. Those who carry out their duty according to my injunctions and those who follow these teachings faithfully will be free from bondage of work. And those who disobey will never reach perfection. Even learned people have desires to sense objects and act under their natural instincts. Detachment to sense objects for self-realisation should be voluntary, not through repression or regulation.

Carry out your prescribed duty even if it is faulty and leads you to destruction.

Arjuna:

What is it that compels a person to engage in sinful acts?

Krishna:

It is desire (*kama*) that generates anger (*krodha*) which in turn generates illusion (*moha*). That is what drives one to engage in sinful acts. As fire is covered by smoke, a mirror is covered by dust and an embryo is covered by the womb, material life is covered by desire. Even knowledge of the learned is covered by desire. It is never satisfied and keeps burning like fire. Desire overpowers mind, senses and even intelligence of a person. Therefore, as the first step in the effort for self-realisation, the senses should be regulated and desire overcome.

I first narrated this everlasting principle (*yoga*) to the Sun God (Vivaswan). The Sun God narrated it to Manu and Manu to Ikswaku. The tradition, thus carried on through the sage kings, seems to have got lost somewhere on the way in course of time. Now, I am repeating it to you as my friend and devotee so that you will understand the secret of this principle.

Arjuna:

How come you narrated it to the Sun God who by age is much senior to you?

Krishna:

Many, many lives you and I had in the past. While I can remember them, you are unable to do so. In my original form, I have no birth and death. But, through my internal energy, I can manifest myself in any form, anywhere, any time. Wherever and whenever moral and ethical standards deteriorate, I manifest myself for the deliverance of those following the righteous path, annihilation of those gone astray and re-establishment of lost values. And this happens in every millennium (*yuga*).

Those who realise the divinity of my manifestation and activities will, after death, enter my abode straight and will have no rebirth. Freed from attachment, fear and anger, being fully absorbed in me and taking refuge in me, many in the past became purified in their knowledge about me, and they developed transcendental love for me thereafter.

People follow my path in all respects. Whichever way they approach me, I reward them for their endeavour. In the material world, people engage themselves in their duty, looking for quick success in their efforts, and, with their prayers to demigods, realise their goal.

I created the fourfold division in society (*varna dharma*). Even though I am its creator, I do not belong to it because of my non-performing and unchanging nature (*akartaram, avyayam*). I am not affected by work or its results. One who understands this truth about me does not get entangled in work and its reaction. All liberated souls of ancient times proceeded with this understanding. You should also perform your duty following in their footsteps.

Even the intelligent get confused about action and inaction. The intricacies of action (*karma*), incorrect action (*vikarma*) and inaction (*akarma*) are difficult to grasp. One should know properly what action is. I shall explain to you what constitutes action. If you know this, you will be liberated from all misfortunes.

A person who can see inaction in action and action in inaction is intellectually at a higher level even though engaged in all sorts of activities like others. One whose endeavour is free from desire for sense gratification and who is always satisfied and independent, even though engaged in any activity, is a non-doer.

A person who, without any desire for the results of work or for possession, performs work only for the bare necessities of life is free from sinful reaction. A person who is satisfied with whatever result comes of its own accord, who has surpassed duality, who is free from envy and who is steady in success and failure is never entangled in work. Detached from material environment, concentrated in transcendental knowledge and performing duty as a sacrifice (*yajna*), one elevates oneself to total transcendence. Such a person merges with the Absolute Truth (*Brahman*) in the end, and whatever duty is performed by that person becomes spiritual in nature.

Some perform sacrifice (*yajna*) for temporary material gains while some others perform it for transcendental knowledge. Some exercise control over their senses through concentration (hearing only what is required to be heard) while some others restrain senses from excessive indulgence in material pleasures.

Those seeking self-realisation control their senses by withdrawing interest in all sense objects (renunciation). By distributing their wealth in charity, undertaking an austere way of life, going through mystic practices (*yoga*) and studying the *Vedas* for advancement of transcendental knowledge, people have gained enlightenment. There are others who, by controlling breathing (*pranayama*) or by controlling food, go into a trance and seek transcendental knowledge. All these sacrifices cleanse sinful reactions and lead one to the path of enlightenment. All of them are approved by the *Vedas* and are born out of different types of duty. If you know this, you will be liberated. Sacrifice performed in knowledge is better than sacrifice performed for material gains.

Present life is an opportunity to disengage from bondage and reach eternal happiness through one's own efforts. If you miss this opportunity, you can never be happy.

All sacrifices (*yajna*) ultimately culminate in transcendental knowledge. A spiritual master can impart this knowledge unto you if you approach him submissively and serve him. Once you obtain this transcendental knowledge, you will be free from all illusions (*maya*), and will realise that all living beings are part of the Supreme (*Parabrahmma*) that is Me. Even if you are the most sinful of sinners, once you attain this transcendental knowledge, you will be able to cross the ocean of miseries.

Knowledge destroys reaction of deeds as fire reduces firewood to ashes. There is nothing comparable with transcendental knowledge. And one who attains this knowledge through devotional service enjoys it within oneself and soon reaches the stage of spiritual peace. For a person who does not believe in this, there is no peace in this world or elsewhere.

One who performs duty as devotional service, who is not concerned with the result of deeds, who overcomes doubts through transcendental knowledge is a self-realised person. Such a person is not bound by reactions of duty. Remove your ignorance through this understanding and perform your duty.

Arjuna:

First you asked me to renounce work. Then you ask me to perform duty as devotional service. Please tell me clearly which one is better.

Krishna:

Both are paths leading to self-realisation. But, of the two, devotional service is better. He who performs duty without looking for the result of his work is a detached person (*sanyasi*). Free from dualities, such a person overcomes material bondage and is totally liberated. Only the ill-informed think that analytical study (*Sankhya*) is different from devotional service (*karma yoga*). Learned people know that the desired result can be attained either way, and those who see these two at the same level see things as they are.

Mere renunciation cannot make one happy. But devotional service can take a learned person to the Supreme (*Brahman*) without any delay. A pure soul who has controlled senses and who is engaged in devotional service is compassionate to all living entities and, though engaged in work, never gets entangled in it. Even if engaged in normal activities such as seeing, hearing, smelling, eating, or moving about, such a person knows that he or she is not doing anything because his or her divine consciousness remains aloof from these activities. Those who perform duty without attachment, leaving results to the Supreme, are unaffected by sinful reactions like the lotus leaf untouched by water.

An enlightened person (*yogi*) abandons attachment to sense gratification and performs duty with body, mind, intelligence and senses only for self-purification. Such a person attains everlasting peace while a person working for the fruits of labour gets entangled. When senses are controlled, the soul (*atman*) resides happily in the material body and neither creates activities nor induces people to act; it is not responsible for the result either. All these are attributable to material nature (*swabhav*).The Supreme

Lord (*Vibhu*) is not responsible for sinful or pious deeds of living beings. Ignorance prevents people from understanding this fact. When ignorance is removed by true knowledge, one can see this truth clearly.

When one's intelligence, mind and faith are fixed in the Supreme, one becomes fully cleansed of misgivings through complete knowledge and proceeds straight to self-realisation. A self-realised person does not recognise any difference in living beings, is steady in happiness and unhappiness, is flawless and merges with *Brahman* through transcendental knowledge. In that state, such a person enjoys everlasting spiritual happiness. Material pleasures and miseries are short-lived and have no appeal to such a person.

A person who can control desire and anger generated from sensual urges and work for the welfare of living beings is a happy person and a real mystic (*yogi*) qualified to merge with the Supreme after death as a liberated soul.

Discarding all doubts, controlling sense organs and concentrating on the Supreme, perform your prescribed duty. You will be free from reactions of work and will enjoy peace within yourself.

A person who performs duty without expecting results is the true *sanyasi* or *yogi*, not the person who does not light a fire or does not perform duty (*kriya*). One who does not renounce desire for sense gratification can never become a *sanyasi*. Renunciation (*sanyasa*) is the same as *yoga*.

For a beginner in the *yoga* system work is the means while a person advanced in that system having renounced desire for sense gratification does not engage in any result-oriented activity.

Our mind (*atmana*) is both friend and enemy of the soul (*atmanam*). Mind should deliver the soul entangled in sense gratification, not degrade it by getting more and more entangled. For a person who has conquered mind, mind is a friend, but for a person who has failed to do it, mind will be an enemy. A person who conquers mind reaches the transcendental stage (*Paramatma*) and enjoys perfect tranquillity. For such a person, heat and cold, happiness and distress, honour and dishonour are all the same. A person who acquires or realises true knowledge (*jnani*) is self-controlled and is situated in transcendence. Such a person does not see any difference in material objects. For a person advanced in the effort for self-realisation, friends and enemies, well-wishers and envious people, sinners and pious people are all alike.

A *yogi* withdraws into seclusion and concentrates on the Supreme in complete self-control and without any attachment to material objects or sense gratification. That is the way to cleanse the mind and prepare a person to become one with the Absolute through meditation (*dhyana yoga*). Such a person becomes free from the cycle of birth and death and merges with the Absolute on cessation of material existence.

It is not necessary for a person to give up food and sleep altogether to become a *yogi*. However, one who takes up *yoga as a* practice should avoid overindulgence in eating and sleeping. Regulated habits help a person to advance on this path without difficulty. When one advances thus, mind gets disciplined and is able to detach from material pleasures and sense gratification. With a controlled mind, a *yogi* remains steady in meditation like a flame in a windless environment. *Yoga* practice should be followed with determination and faith. With self-control and concentration, one must move on to the objective of self-realisation.

Having reached the stage of trance (*samadhi*) with the help of *yoga*, the purified mind sees the real self and rejoices in the transcendental happiness which this experience brings. The *yogi* will then know that there is no greater gain than that, and that will be the end of all miseries and unhappiness affecting material life.

Mind, by its very nature, is flickering and unsteady. A self-realised *yogi* brings it back whenever it strays and keeps it under control. With a completely controlled mind, the *yogi* realises identity with the Absolute, attains eternal happiness and is free from all sinful reactions. In such a state, the *yogi* sees self in all living beings and all living beings in self.

For one who sees me everywhere and sees everything in me, I am not lost, nor is that person lost to me. Worshipping me with this knowledge, such a person always resides with me and sees the true equality of all living beings in their happiness and distress.

Arjuna:

I am unable to understand the yoga system which you propounded now because of my unsteady mind. Controlling a flickering and obstinate mind appears to me more difficult than controlling air.

Krishna:

Undoubtedly, it is difficult to control a restless mind. However, I feel that it is possible to do so through suitable practice and detachment.

Arjuna:

What happens to a person who begins yoga with faith and determination but who deviates later due to worldly pressures and thereby becomes unsuccessful in the effort for self-realisation? Will such a person perish like a shattered cloud without material or spiritual success and without a position anywhere? This is my doubt. No one other than you can remove this doubt.

Krishna:

One who engages in auspicious activities will never meet with destruction either in this life or the next. No evil can befall good work. The unsuccessful *yogi* will get a better opportunity to remove the causes of his failure in the next life. By reviving progress made in the past life and making further efforts in the present life, the failed *yogi* can reach perfection. By virtue of the divine consciousness of previous life, such a *yogi* takes to *yoga* principles automatically and, with determined effort, becomes successful ultimately.

I shall tell you how a person who performs *yoga* with mind attached to me and fully dependent on me can know my real self. Once you know this, nothing more will be left for you to know. One in a million alone will have this rare privilege of knowing me in full.

Earth, water, fire, air, ether, mind, intelligence and self-assertion constitute the eightfold manifestations of my energy. Above them stands the manifestation of my superior energy, the living entities. All creations have their origin in these two energies, and I am the source of their origin and annihilation. I am the Ultimate Truth, and everything rests on me. I am the light of the Sun and the Moon, the syllable 'Om' in sacred verse (*mantra*); I am sound, I am ability in man. I am the fragrance of the earth, heat in fire, life in all lives and penances of all ascetics. I am the original seed of existence, intelligence of the intelligent and prowess of all-powerful men. I am the strength of the strong, devoid of passion and desire. I am sex life which is not contrary to religious principles.

All the states of being – goodness (*satwa guna*), passion (*rajo guna*) and ignorance (*tamo guna*) – are the manifestations of my energy. Yet, I am independent of them. Deluded by these three states, the whole world does not see me who am above them and inexhaustible. This illusory energy (*maya*) of mine is difficult to overcome. But those who surrender to me can do it. Only those who do not want to look beyond the material world refuse to surrender.

Those who are devoted to me fall under four categories – the distressed, the seekers of wealth, the inquisitive and those wanting to know the absolute. Of these, those who are in the full knowledge of me and who are engaged in pure devotional service are special, for I am near to them, and they are dear to me. All are, no doubt, magnanimous souls, but those who are in the know of my real self are like myself. Being engaged in devotional service to me, they are sure to reach me, the highest and most perfect goal. After many births and deaths, the one who is in the know of my real self surrenders to me, knowing that I am present in everything. Such a person is rare.

Those who are deprived of this knowledge by their material attachment render their devotional service to those conceived by them as Gods according to the rules of worship designed by their nature. I encourage them and help them to follow their faith steadily. Whatever they achieve through such worship is also, in the ultimate analysis, granted by me. However, their goal is limited and temporary. But my devotees reach the supreme goal of merging with me forever.

Ordinary people see me only in this material form. Due to their limited understanding, they are unable to see my imperishable, impersonal, and supreme form. I am not manifest for those living in the illusory world, and they cannot, therefore, see that I am unborn and inexhaustible. I know everything that has happened in the past, all that is happening in the present and all that is yet to happen. And no one knows me.

All living beings struggle in this illusory world dominated by desire and hate. People who follow the path of righteousness in life and whose sins are eradicated are free from this delusion, and they engage in devotional service to me with determination. For liberation from old age and death, they take refuge in me. They are aware of all transcendental activities. Knowing me as the be-all and end-all of this universe, these men hold on to me even at the time of their death.

Arjuna:

What is *Brahmma*? What is *adhyatma*? What is *karma*? What is *adhibhutam*? What is *adhidaivam*? Please explain. Who is the Lord of sacrifice (*yajna*), and how does he live in the body of a living being? How can a person engaged in devotional service know you at the time of death?

Krishna:

The indestructible transcendental living entity is *Brahmma*, and its eternal nature is *adhyatma*. Action originating from material consciousness of the living being is *karma*. Physical nature which constantly changes is *adhibhutam* (material manifestation). Universal form of the Lord is *adhidaivata*. And I, the Supreme Lord and the soul in every embodied being, am *adhi yajna* (Lord of sacrifice).

Whatever state of being one has in mind at the time of death, one reaches that state after quitting the body. He who remembers me at the time of his death reaches me certainly. Therefore, keep your mind fixed on me always, and you will reach me certainly. Anyone who is steady in this path is sure to reach me. Always imagine me as the one who knows everything, who is the oldest, who is the controller, who is smaller than the smallest, who is the maintainer of everything, who is beyond all material conception, who is like the Sun in darkness and who is transcendental.

He who brings his life between the eyebrows with powers obtained through *yoga* training and dies with an undeviating mind fixed in the Supreme will certainly reach the Supreme. Those well-versed in the *Vedas* enter the stage of *Brahmman* by chanting the syllable 'Om'. Desiring perfection, some practice celibacy. I shall explain briefly the process for attaining salvation (*moksha*).

At the time of death, a person trained in *yoga* controls his senses and brings his mind to the heart and life on top of his head. In that posture, chanting the syllable 'Om' and keeping his mind fixed on the absolute, he takes his last breath, and the liberated soul merges with the Supreme. For those who remember me always and are engaged in my devotional service, I am close to them. After reaching me, they do not have to go back to this world of miseries through rebirth because they have attained perfection.

By human calculation, a thousand ages (*yuga*) taken together form one day of *Brahmma*. Same is the case with night. At the beginning of *Brahma's* day all living entities become manifest, and at the end of that day they merge with the unmanifested. This process continues with repeated births and deaths of living entities during the manifested stage. Yet there is another unmanifested nature which is eternal and transcendental. That is the Supreme which is never annihilated even when all manifested beings are annihilated.

That which is described as unmanifested and infallible, that which is known as the ultimate destination, that place from which no one returns after arrival – that is the abode of the Supreme. While being present in this abode, He is all-pervading, and everything is situated within Him. Through pure devotion, one can reach the Supreme.

There is a belief that if a person dies at an auspicious time of the year like a day in the waxing Moon period (*shukla paksha*) or during the Sun's northward journey (*uttarayana*) that person's soul will reach the Supreme, while death on a day during the waning Moon period (*krishna paksha*) or during the Sun's southward journey (*dakshinayana*) will result in that person's rebirth. There is also the belief that if one passes away during daytime, one does not come back, while one returns if the death is at night. Devotees know these sayings, but they are not bewildered. A person who follows the path of devotion can reap the rewards that others may derive from knowledge of the Vedas, austere sacrifices, charities, or analytical studies (*Sankhya*).

Now, I shall impart the most confidential knowledge knowing which you will be relieved of the miseries of material existence. It is the King of education, the secret of all secrets and the purest knowledge. It is the direct realisation of self, perfect religion and everlasting. Those who are not faithful in this devotional service cannot reach me and have to come back to the path of birth and death in this material world.

The entire universe is pervaded by me in my unmanifested form. But I am not in them; nor does this creation of mine rest in me. Although I am the maintainer of all living entities, and although I am everywhere, I am not part of this cosmic manifestation because I am the source of this creation. As the mighty wind blowing everywhere rests in the sky, all created beings, wherever they are, ultimately rest in me. At the end of a millennium (*yuga*), all material manifestations return to me only to be recreated at the beginning of the next millennium.

The whole cosmic order is under me. Under my will, it is automatically manifested and annihilated again and again. All this work cannot bind me. Although neutral, I am never detached from these activities. The animate and inanimate objects manifest and unmanifest under my supervision.

When I manifest in human form, ignorant people take me for granted without knowing that I am the Supreme Lord of the universe. In that condition, all their hope, their effort and their knowledge lead them only to failure. On the other hand, great souls shielded by their divine nature engage in devotional service, knowing my original and inexhaustible nature. Chanting my glories, endeavouring with determination, bowing down before me, these great souls worship me always.

People worship me in different ways. There are some who worship me through cultivated knowledge. Some others do that through sacrifices (*yajna*). Some believe in my oneness, while some believe in duality. And there are others who consider me in my universal form. I am all these. I exist everywhere and in everything. I take care of those who worship me with single-minded devotion. Those who worship God in other names are, in fact, worshipping me, although in a wrong way. I am the enjoyer and master of all sacrifices (*yajna*). Those who worship me in my real form remain with me, while those who do not understand my real form fall down. Whatever is offered to me, be it a leaf, a flower, a fruit or water, with love and devotion, I accept it. Whatever you do, do it as an offering to me. That will free you from bondage of work and auspicious or inauspicious results. Thus liberated, you will come to me.

I am equally disposed to all. Those who worship me with devotion are with me as I am with them. What would appear as a crime will also be condoned if it is done as part of devotional service. My devotee never perishes but attains everlasting peace. Those who take shelter in me can attain the supreme destination irrespective of sex or caste. Having come to this temporary world of miseries, through their devotional service, they can reach me. Always engage your mind in thinking of me, in worshipping me. Being completely absorbed in me, you will reach me.

Neither the demigods (*suragana*) nor the sages (*rishis*) know my origin. In every respect, I am their source. Only one who knows me as the unborn, the beginningless, and the Supreme Lord will, being the undeluded, be freed from all sins. Intelligence, knowledge, freedom from doubt and delusion, forgiveness, truthfulness, control of senses and mind, happiness, birth, death, fear, fearlessness, non-violence, equanimity, satisfaction, austerity, charity, fame, and notoriety are created by me alone. The seven sages, the four sages before them and the Manu family were born out of me, and from them came the existing population.

Those who come to know me in this opulence and powers, who know that I am the source of spiritual and material worlds and that everything emanates from me, will undoubtedly engage in my devotional service with all their heart. Their thoughts dwell on me, and they derive satisfaction in exchanging ideas about me with like-minded people. To them, I grant them the understanding to reach me. As a gesture of mercy, I, dwelling in their hearts, destroy their darkness born out of ignorance with the shining lamp of knowledge.

Arjuna:

You are the ultimate truth, the eternal transcendental original person, the unborn and the greatest. So say the great sages Narada, Asita, Devala, and Vyasa. And now you are yourself declaring that to me. I accept it totally as the truth. Neither the demigods nor the asuras can understand you. Indeed, you alone know yourself through your internal potency. Please tell me in detail about the divine opulence by which you pervade the world. How shall I constantly think of you? How shall I know you? In what forms are you to be remembered? Please describe the mystic power of your opulence. I am never satiated to hear about you. The more I hear, the more I want to hear and taste the nectar of your words.

Krishna:

All right, I shall now speak to you about my divine opulence, but only those which are prominent because my opulence is unlimited.

I am the soul in all living entities, the beginning, the middle and the end of all beings, I am Vishnu among Suns, radiant Sun among lights, Marichi among wind, Moon among stars; *Sama Veda* among *Vedas*, Indra among demigods, mind among senses, and consciousness among living beings; Shiva among Rudras, lord of wealth among *yakshas* and *rakshasas*, fire among *vasus* and Meru among mountains; Brihaspati among priests, Skanda among generals, and ocean among water bodies; Bhrigu among sages, *Om* (*ekamaksharam*) among vibrations, chanting of holy names among sacrifices (*yajna*) and Himalaya among the immovable; banyan tree among trees, Narada among demigod sages, Chitraratha among Gandharvas and Kapila among perfected sages; Uchaisravas among horses, Airavat among elephants and king among men; Vajra among weapons, Surabhi (*kamadhuk*) among cows, Kandarpa (demigod of love) in procreation and Vasuki among serpents; Anantha among snakes, Varuna among aquatic beings, Aryama among ancestors and Yama among dispensers of law; Prahlada among demons, time among subduers, lion among animals and Garuda among birds; wind among purifiers, Rama among wielders of weapons, shark among fish and Ganga among rivers; the beginning, the middle and the end of all creations, spiritual education among education, conclusion among discussions; first letter (*akara*) among letters, dual in the compound, inexhaustible in time and creator of Brahmma (*viswathomukha*); I am the all-devouring death and origin of future. Among women, I am fame, beauty, memory, intelligence, steadfastness, and patience. Of *Sama Veda*, I am *Brihat Sama*, *Gayatri* among sacred verses (*mantras*), *Margashirsha* (November-December) among the months of the year and spring among the seasons. I am the gambling of cheats, the splendour of the splendid, success of entrepreneurs and strength of the strong. I am Vasudeva among Vrishni, Dhananjaya (Arjuna) among Pandavas, Vyasa among sages and Usana among poets, punishment among lawlessness, morality among the victorious, silence in secrets and wisdom among the wise. I am the generating seed of all existence. No animate or inanimate entity can exist without me.

There is no end to my divine manifestations. What I have told you is only a mere indication. All the beautiful creations spring from a spark of my splendour. Where is the necessity for this detailed knowledge? With a fragment of myself, I support the entire universe.

Arjuna:

What you have told me has dispelled all my illusions. I have heard from you in detail about the appearance and disappearance of all living entities and have realised your inexhaustible glories. Now, I wish to see you in your cosmic form if you think I can see that unlimited universal form.

Krishna:

Arjuna, See me now in my hundreds and thousands of varied and multi-coloured forms; see the different manifestations of Aditya, Vasu, Rudra, Aswinikumara and other demigods. Behold all these which had not been seen or heard before. This universal form can show you whatever you wish to see and whatever you may want to see in future. You cannot see them with your mortal eyes. I will, therefore, give you divine sight.

(Saying this, Krishna displayed his universal form to Arjuna. Arjuna could see in that form unlimited mouths, unlimited eyes, unlimited wonderful visions; celestial ornaments, garments and raised weapons; divine scents emitting from the body. All were beyond explanation. His effulgence was more than that of a thousand Suns; unlimited expanse of the universe situated in one place. Bewildered and astonished, Arjuna bowed his head and began praying to the Supreme Lord)

Arjuna:

Lord, I see assembled in your body all demigods and other living entities. I see Brahma sitting on the lotus flower. I see Siva and all great sages. I see the divine serpents. I see in you many bellies, mouths and eyes expanded everywhere. I see no beginning, middle or end. I see your glowing form with crowns, clubs and discs. I see you as blazing fire or as the radiance of the Sun. Now I realise that you are the basis of the universe, you are inexhaustible, you are the maintainer of the eternal religion (*Sanatanadharma)*, and you are the Supreme God. You have no beginning or end, and, with your radiance, you keep the universe alive and warm. Seeing your terrible form spread throughout, the three worlds are trembling. All demigods are surrendering and entering you, some of them frightened and offering prayers with folded hands. Great sages and perfected beings are singing the Vedic hymns and praying to you. All the manifestations of Siva, all forefathers, *gandharvas, yakshas* and *asuras* are watching your form with wonder. Seeing your terrible form, like others, I am also perturbed. I am unable to maintain my steadiness. Have mercy on me, Lord. I see the sons of Dritarashtra, Bhishma, Drona, Karna, and other chieftains entering your mouth, some of them getting smashed by your teeth. They are entering your mouth as moths rush to a blazing fire or as rivers flow into the ocean. All of them are being devoured by you. Lord, please tell me who you are and what your mission is.

Krishna:

I am time. I am the destroyer. All those assembled here other than you (Pandavas) will be slain by me. You are only the instrument for my mission. Get up and fight. Destroy your enemies and enjoy victory and a flourishing kingdom. Warriors like Bhishma, Drona, Jayadratha, and Karna have already lost. Do not be disturbed by that. You fight and be victorious.

Arjuna:

Lord, the whole world enjoys hearing your name, and they become attached to you. Enlightened ones pay respectful homage to you while wrongdoers flee from you. You are the cause of all causes, the imperishable, and the refuge of all. You are the knower of everything, and you are all that is knowable. You pervade the whole cosmic manifestation. You are the air, fire and water; you are the Moon. I offer my obeisance a thousand times unto you. Without knowing your real form, I have behaved with you as a friend. Please forgive me if I have behaved incorrectly due to my ignorance. As a father tolerating the impudence of his son, as a person tolerating the impertinence of a friend, I pray to you to tolerate me. Also, please come back to your mortal form, as this universal form is frightening. I wish to see you with conch, wheel, mace and lotus in your four hands.

Krishna:

Happily have I shown you my universal form through my internal potency. No one has seen it before you. Study of *Vedas*, performing of sacrifices (yajna), charity, pious action, and penance cannot help anyone in this material world to see this form. By seeing this form, you are perturbed. I shall come back to my normal form now so that you can see me as you wish to see me.

Arjuna:

Seeing you in your normal form, my anxieties have disappeared.

Krishna:

Only through undivided devotional service can I be understood. Those who engage in my devotional service without any self-interest or speculation, who make me the goal of life and who are friendly to every living being shall certainly understand me and ultimately merge with me.

Arjuna:

Who is considered more perfect? Those who engage themselves in your devotional service? Or those who worship the impersonal, unmanifested *Brahmman?*

Krishna:

Those who fix their mind on my personal form and are engaged in my worship with transcendental faith (*bhakti yogis*) are more perfect. For them, I am the swift deliverer from the ocean of birth and death. Those who are engaged in worshipping me in my unmanifested, impersonal form (*jnana yogis*), controlling senses and engaging in the welfare of all, also reach me in the end. Their progress will, however, be slow and troublesome. Therefore, fix your mind upon me always (*bhakti yoga*), and you will always be with me. If you are unable to do this, then follow the regulatory principles of *bhakti yoga* and develop a desire to reach me. If you are unable to do that, perform your duty as a devotional service for me (*karma yoga*). By doing that, you will reach the perfect stage. In the event of your inability to do this, try to act by giving up all expectations of the results of your work (*nishkama karma*) and try to be self-situated. If all these methods are difficult for you, think of cultivating knowledge (*jnana yoga*). However, better than knowledge is meditation and better than meditation is work without expectation of result. One can attain peace of mind through *nishkama karma*.

One who is a kind friend to all living entities, who is not envious, who does not possess any proprietorship on anything, who is free from false ego, who is equal in happiness and distress, who is tolerant, satisfied and self-controlled, who engages in devotional service with determination, who has mind and intelligence fixed on me – such a devotee is very dear to me.

Arjuna:

I want to know about nature (*Prakrti*) and enjoyer (*Purusha*), field (*kshetra*) and knower of the field (*kshetrajna*), knowledge (*jnanam*) and the object of knowledge (*jneyam*).

Krishna:

This body is the field and one who knows it is the knower of the field. Understanding the body and its knower is knowledge. I am also the knower of bodies. Knowledge of the field and knower of the field is described by sages in various *Vedic* writings, particularly in *Vedanta Sutra* with all reasoning as to cause and effect.

The five elements – false ego, intelligence, the unmanifested, the ten senses and the mind, and the five sense objects – desire, hatred, happiness, distress and the aggregate life symptoms and convictions are considered to be the field of activities and its interactions. Humility, absence of pride, non-violence, tolerance, simplicity, respect for spiritual guide, cleanliness, steadiness, self-control, renunciation of objects of sense gratification, absence of false ego, clear perception of birth, death, old age and disease, detachment, freedom from entanglement with children, wife and home, even-mindedness amid pleasant and unpleasant events, devotion to God, aspiring to a solitary life, detachment from the mass of people, accepting the importance of self-realisation and search for the absolute truth – all these I declare as knowledge. Other than these, whatever there can be is ignorance.

I shall now explain the knowable, knowing which you will taste nectar (*amritam*). The beginningless *Brahmma*, subordinate to me, is beyond cause and effect. He pervades everything with his hands, legs, heads, faces, and eyes. He exists inside and outside of all living beings, the moving and the unmoving. Because he is subtle, he cannot be seen or known in the material sense. Although far away, he is also near to everyone. Although he appears to be divided among all beings, he is never divided. He is the maintainer of all. But it is to be understood that he devours and develops all. He is the light in luminous objects and is beyond the darkness of matter. He is knowledge, the object of knowledge and the goal of knowledge (*jnana gamyam*). He is situated in everyone's heart.

I have briefly explained the fields of activity (*kshetra*), knowledge (*jnanam*), and knowable (*jneyam*) to you. Only my devotees can understand this and thus attain my nature. Material nature (*prakrti*) and living beings (*purusha*) are without beginning. Their transformation and modes are produced by material nature. Nature is said to be the cause of all causes and effects, whereas the living entity is the cause of enjoyment and suffering. Living beings situated in material nature and associated with the modes of nature have to face good and bad aspects of nature. Yet, a super soul (*paramatma*) resides in the body of the living beings as the master, overseer and transcendental enjoyer. One who understands this philosophy concerning material nature, the living entity, and the modes of nature, regardless of one's present position, is sure to attain liberation from the cycle of birth and death. Some see the super soul within themselves through meditation (*dhyana yoga*), some through the cultivation of knowledge (*jnana yoga*), some through philosophical discussion (*sankhya*) and some others through the performance of duty without expectation of results (*karma yoga*). Again, there are people who, although not conversant with spiritual knowledge, begin to worship the Supreme by listening to others (*bhakti yoga*). They also succeed in transcending the cycle of birth and death.

Whatever is seen in existence, moving or stationary, is nothing but a combination of the field (*kshetra*) and the knower of the field (*kshetrajna*). One who sees the super soul (*paramatma*) in all destructible bodies and who understands that soul is indestructible actually sees, and one who sees the super soul equally present everywhere without any feeling of degradation of mind approaches the transcendental destination. Such a person would attain spiritual vision and see that all the work done is by the body and not by the soul. The soul, although situated in the body, never gets entangled in the work done by the body. Like the Sun illuminating the world, the soul illuminates the body by consciousness. Those who understand the difference between the body and the knower of the body and the process of liberation from bondage in material nature will reach the supreme goal.

Now, I shall disclose to you the supreme wisdom, the best of all knowledge, knowing which sages attained transcendental perfection. By becoming fixed in this knowledge, one can attain a transcendental nature like mine. Thus established, one is not born at the time of creation or disturbed at the time of dissolution.

I produce living entities through *Brahmma*, the source of birth. I am the seed-giving father of all species that give birth in material nature. The eternal living entity (*atma*) in the material body, coming in contact with nature, is conditioned by three modes – goodness (*satwa guna*), passion (*rajo guna*) and ignorance (*tamo guna*). The mode of goodness (*satwa guna*), being purer than the other two, illuminates and frees one from all sinful reactions. Those conditioned by this mode live in happiness and wisdom. The mode of passion (*rajo guna*) is born of desires and longings, and hence, the living entity conditioned by this mode is tied down to result-oriented activities. The mode of ignorance (*tamo guna*) is the delusion of living entities, which leads to madness, indolence, and sleeplessness. There is a tendency for the three modes to compete among themselves for supremacy.

Manifestation of the mode of goodness (*satwa guna*) can be experienced when all gates of the material body are illuminated by knowledge. Attachment, uncontrollable desire, and intense result-oriented activity are the symptoms of the mode of passion (*rajo guna*). Illusion, darkness, inertia, and madness result from an excess of the mode of ignorance (*tamo guna*). When one dies in the mode of goodness, one reaches higher levels of existence. When one dies in the mode of passion, one takes rebirth among similarly oriented living entities. The person dying in ignorance takes rebirth among the animal species. The result of action done in the mode of goodness is pure, but action done in the mode of passion leads to misery, while action done in the mode of ignorance is foolish. From the mode of goodness develops knowledge; from the mode of passion develops greed; from the mode of ignorance develops illusion, madness, and foolishness.

Those in the mode of goodness go up to higher levels, those in the mode of passion remain where they are, and those in the mode of ignorance go still further down. When a person understands this truth and also knows that the Supreme Lord is above all the three modes, that person attains spiritual perfection. When the embodied being (*Atma*) is able to transcend the three modes associated with the material body, that being gets liberated from the cycle of birth and death, old age and unhappiness and can attain perpetual happiness.

Arjuna:

By which symptom is a person who has risen above these three modes known? What will that person's behaviour be, and how does that person transcend those modes?

Krishna:

He who does not hate illumination, attachment and delusion when they are present or does not long for them when they disappear; who is unwavering and undisturbed by reactions of the material qualities; who remains neutral and transcendental knowing that the modes alone are active; who is situated in the self and considers happiness and distress alike; who looks upon a lump of earth, a stone and a piece of gold with an equal eye; who is equal to the desirable and undesirable; who is steady and accepts praise and blame, honour and dishonour equally; who treats friend and enemy alike, and who has renounced all material activity is the person who is said to have transcended the three modes of nature. One who engages in full devotional service, unfailing in all circumstances, transcends the modes of material nature and reaches the level of *Brahmman*. And I am the basis of the impersonal *Brahmman*, immortal, imperishable, eternal and the position of ultimate happiness.

It is said that there is an eternal banyan tree with its roots upward (*oordhwa moolam*) and branches downward (*adho shakha*). Its leaves are the *Vedic* hymns. He who knows this is the knower of the *Vedas*. The branches of this tree extend downward and upward, nourished by the three modes (*guna*) of material nature. Twigs (*pravala*) are the sense objects. The tree also has roots going down, bound by the deeds of the material world. The real form of this tree cannot be perceived in this world. No one can understand where its foundation is, where it begins or where it ends. With determination, one must cut down this strongly rooted tree with the weapon of detachment. Thereafter, one must seek that place from which, having gone, one never returns. Having reached that place, one must surrender to the Supreme power from whom everything began and extended through the ages.

Those who are free from false sense of prestige, illusion, and false association, who understand the eternal, who overcome lust, who are freed from the duality of happiness and distress and who, unbewildered, know how to surrender to the Supreme power reach that eternal stage (*Padam*). That abode is not illumined by the Sun, Moon, or fire. Those who reach it never return.

Living entities in this world are my eternal fragmented parts. Due to their conditioned life, they struggle hard with their six senses including the mind during their life span. From one material body to another, the soul moves carrying experiences and conceptions of life like the wind carrying aroma and shapes the new body on the basis of such experiences and conceptions.

An ignorant person cannot understand this. But a self-realised person or an eye trained in knowledge can see all this.

The splendour of the Sun, Moon and fire emanate from me. By using my energy, I sustain all living and non-living objects. I make life possible in living beings. I am seated in every heart. From me come remembrance, forgetfulness, and knowledge. I am to be known through the *Vedas*. I am the compiler of the *Vedanta*; I am the knower of the *Vedas*.

There are two classes of living beings -- the fallible and the infallible. In the material world, everyone is fallible, whereas everyone in the spiritual world is infallible. Besides these two, there is the greatest living personality, the Supreme soul (*Paramatma*), the imperishable Lord who maintains the three worlds. I am celebrated as the Supreme Lord because I am transcendental and beyond both the fallible and the infallible. Whoever knows me as the Supreme Lord, without any doubt, is the knower of everything. He engages himself in my full devotional service.

This is the most confidential part of the Vedic revelations, and I have disclosed this to you. Whoever understands this will become wise and attain perfection in his endeavours.

Fearlessness, purification of one's existence, cultivation of spiritual knowledge, charity, self-control, performance of sacrifice (*yajna*), study of the *Vedas*, austerity, simplicity, non-violence, truthfulness, freedom from anger, renunciation, tranquillity, aversion to fault-finding, compassion to all living beings, freedom from covetousness, gentleness, modesty, steady determination, vigour, forgiveness, fortitude, cleanliness, freedom from envy and freedom from passion for honour –

these transcendental qualities belong to godly men endowed with divine nature. Pride, arrogance, conceit, anger, harshness, and ignorance – these qualities belong to those with a demonic (*asura*) nature. Transcendental qualities lead to liberation, while the demonic qualities lead to bondage. Do not worry, Arjuna, you are born with divine qualities.

In this world, there are two types of creations -- divine and demonic. I have told you about the divine at length. Now, hear more about the demonic from me. They do not know what is to be done or not to be done. Cleanliness, proper behaviour and truth are not found in them. For them, the world is unreal, with no foundation, with no supernatural power in control, arisen without any cause and is supported only by desire. With such belief, these people engage themselves in unbeneficial and horrible work to destroy the world. Based on such ideas, their pride and insatiable desire guide their unclean work under illusion. They believe that gratification of the senses is the prime purpose of life. They live under immeasurable anxiety till the end of their life. Bound by endless desires and absorbed in lust (*kama*) and anger (*krodha*), they accumulate wealth through illegal means for sense gratification. They do it under the illusion that more wealth would bring more happiness. They will eliminate enemies and will feel that they are powerful and happy. They will perform sacrifices and give charity for self-glorification. Such people are deluded by ignorance. Thus, getting more and more attached to enjoyment, they ultimately fall down into hell. Living under false ego, pride, lust, and anger, they become envious of the Super soul residing within them and fall into irreligious ways. Such people have to continue in the material world perpetually with their low forms of life. They sink into abominable existence and can never reach God.

There are three gates leading to self-destruction and hell – lust, anger, and greed. One must give them up. A person who has succeeded in giving them up performs acts conducive to self-realisation and gradual attainment of the supreme destination. He who discards scriptural injunctions and acts according to his own whims and fancies attains neither perfection nor happiness nor the supreme destination. One should, therefore, understand what duty is and what it is not according to the scriptures and act accordingly.

Arjuna:

What about those who do not follow the scriptures but worship in their own way with full faith? Are they in goodness, passion, or ignorance mode?

Krishna:

According to one's existence under the various modes of nature (*satwa*, *rajas* and *tamas*), one's faith evolves. Those in the mode of goodness (*satwa guna*) worship the demigods (*deva gana*); those in the mode of passion (*rajo guna*) worship the demons (*yaksha-rakshas*); those in the mode of ignorance (*tamo guna*) worship ghosts and spirits (*preta-bhuta gana*). Those who, impelled by their lust and attachment or motivated by their ego and pride, undergo severe austerities and penances not recommended in the scriptures are foolish people torturing their bodies and souls, and they are considered demons.

The modes influence even the food consumed. Food preferred by those with good nature (*satwa guna*) is conducive to longevity, health and happiness. Hot, sour, pungent and spicy food is preferred by those with passion (*rajo guna*). Such food causes distress, misery, and disease. Tasteless, putrid, and bad-smelling food is acceptable to those in the ignorant category (*tamo guna*).

Same is the case with sacrifices, austerity, and charity. Sacrifice performed in accordance with the directions of the scriptures and without expectation of reward has the nature of goodness; sacrifice performed with the intention of gaining material benefit or for the sake of pride fits in with the mode of passion. Any sacrifice performed ignoring the scriptural directives and without faith suits the ignorant mode.

Austerity of the body consists of worship of *devas*, *brahmmanas*, spiritual masters, and elders, as well as cleanliness, simplicity, celibacy, and non-violence. Austerity of speech consists of speaking words that are truthful, pleasing, beneficial and acceptable to others. It also includes regular recitals of *Vedic* literature. Satisfaction, simplicity, self-control, and purification of existence are austerities of the mind. These threefold austerities performed with transcendental faith and without expectation of benefits are collectively called austerity in goodness. Austerity out of pride and for the sake of honour and worship is said to be in the mode of passion. It is neither stable nor permanent. Pretended austerity with self-torture or with the intention of harming others is in the mode of ignorance.

Charity administered out of duty, without expectation of return, at the proper time and place and to a worthy person is in the mode of goodness. But charity given with expectation of some return or for self-gain in some other way or given in a grudging mood is in the mode of passion. Charity given at an impure place, at an improper time, to unworthy persons without respect or proper attention is in the mode of ignorance.

The three words 'Om – tat – sat' were used by *brahmmanas* from early times symbolically indicating the Absolute Truth while chanting the hymns of the *Vedas* or during sacrifices. The transcendentalists, therefore, begin sacrifices, charity and penance with these three words according to scriptural instruction. Those who desire liberation begin sacrifice, penance and charity with the word 'sat' to get free from material entanglement. The objective, the performer, and the activity of sacrifices, penance, and charity are called 'sat' because they are all in the name of the Supreme. Anything done without faith in the Supreme is 'asat' and is of no value in this life or the next.

Arjuna:

I want to know from you the principle of renunciation (*tyaga*) and the renounced order of life (*sanyasa*).

Krishna:

Giving up of activities based on material desire is what learned men call renounced order of life (*sanyasa*). Giving up the results of activities is what wise men call renunciation (*tyaga*).

Some learned men say that all activities are to be abandoned as faulty, while others say that activities like sacrifice (*yajna*), charity (*daana*) and penance (*tapas*) need not be given up. In my opinion, activities like sacrifice, charity, and penance should not be given up. They should be performed as they purify even great men. I would also add that they should be performed without any attachment or expectation of result.

Prescribed duties should never be given up. If you give them up under any illusion, it will be considered an act arising out of ignorance (*tamo guna*). If you give up out of fear or thinking that they are troublesome or are likely to cause bodily discomfort, you will be considered as acting under passion (*rajo guna*). Such action will not lead to elevation. When you perform prescribed duties thinking that they ought to be done, and act without any attachment to or expectation of result, you will be considered as situated in the goodness mode (*satwa guna*) in my opinion. The intelligent renouncer (*thyagi*) situated in goodness mode (*satwa guna*) neither hates inauspicious work nor is attached to auspicious work, and has no doubts about work. It is impossible to give up all activities. But he who renounces the fruits of work is a true renouncer. The threefold results of action – desirable, undesirable, and mixed – accrue after death to a person who is not renounced, but a renounced person is not affected by that.

According to *Vedanta*, there are five causes for accomplishment of all actions. They are the body, the performer, the endeavour, the senses, and the embodied soul. Whatever right or wrong action a person performs by body, mind or speech is caused by these five factors. He who ignores this fact and thinks that he is the doer is unintelligent and cannot see things as they are. He who is not influenced by false ego and whose mind is not bound by attachment, even if he kills people, is not killing them, nor is he bound by his action. Knowledge, the object of knowledge and the knower are the three factors that motivate action; the senses, the work, and the doer are the three constituents of action. According to the three different modes of nature (*satwa, rajas* and *tamas*), there are three different kinds of knowledge, knower and action. Those situated in the mode of goodness (*satwa guna*) see the imperishable soul as one even though it appears as divided in innumerable forms. One who sees the soul only in the distributed form is in the mode of passion (*rajo guna*). One who is attached to one kind of work as the all-in-all without the knowledge of truth is said to be in the mode of darkness (*tamo guna*).

That action, which is regulated, and which is performed without attachment, without love or hatred and without desire for results is said to be in the mode of goodness. Action performed with great effort seeking gratification of desire or performed on the basis of false ego is in the mode of passion. Action performed in illusion, without concern for future bondage or violence caused to others, is said to be in the mode of darkness.

Again, one who performs duty with great enthusiasm and determination without attachment to material nature, without wavering in success and failure, without false ego is in the goodness mode; One who is attached to work and its results, desiring to enjoy the result of that work, greedy, jealous, impure in mind and subject to joy and sorrow is in the passion mode. And one who disregards injunctions of scriptures, who is lazy, indifferent, obstinate, morose, an expert in cheating and insulting others, is in the mode of darkness.

Now listen to what I say about the different kinds of understanding and determination according to the three modes.

That understanding by which one knows what is to be done and what is not to be done, what is to be feared and what is not to be afraid of, what is binding and what is liberation, is in the mode of goodness. The understanding which cannot distinguish between religion and irreligion (*dharma* and *adharma*), between action to be done and action not to be done, is in the mode of passion. The understanding which considers religion to be irreligion and *vice versa*, which guides one in the wrong direction in everything, is in the mode of darkness.

Determination which is unbreakable, sustained with steadfastness achieved through *yoga*, and which controls activities of the mind, life and the senses is determination in the mode of goodness. Determination, which is sustained by a desire for results in work (*karma*), sense gratification (*kama*) or wealth (*artha*), is in the mode of passion. And, determination which cannot go beyond dreaming and is governed by lack of clarity, fearfulness, lamentation, moroseness and illusion is in the mode of darkness.

Now hear from me the three kinds of happiness which one can enjoy and which can take one, through practice, to the end of all distress.

That happiness which may appear like poison in the beginning but may end up like nectar awakening self-realisation is said to be in the mode of goodness. That happiness which one derives through sense gratification and which may appear like nectar in the beginning but end up as poison is said to be in the passion mode. And, that happiness arising out of laziness, delusion or dreaming which is illusory from beginning to end is in the darkness mode.

No living being is free from these three modes born out of material nature. Activities of *brahmmanas, kshatriyas,vaisyas* and *sudras* are distinguished on the basis of their nature determined by these three modes. Peacefulness, self-control, austerity, purity, tolerance, honesty, knowledge, wisdom, and religiosity are the natural qualities of a *brahmmana's* activities. Heroism, power, determination, resourcefulness, courage in battle, generosity and leadership are the natural qualities of activities attributable to a *kshatriya*. While farming, cow-protection and trading are the natural activities of the *vaisyas*, labour and service are those of the *sudras.* By following one's own calling, one can attain perfection. Now I shall tell you how this can be done.

If people perform duties assigned to them as a worship of the Lord who is all-pervasive, they will attain perfection. It is better to perform one's own prescribed duty imperfectly than to perform duties prescribed for others perfectly. Duties prescribed according to one's nature are never affected by sinful reactions. Every endeavour may be covered by some fault, as fire is covered by smoke. One should not give up prescribed duties for that reason. Through self-control, detachment and renunciation one can attain freedom from reaction.

I shall now tell you how such a person can reach *Brahmman*, the absolute truth and knowledge.

One who, with purified intelligence and controlled mind gives up desire for material happiness, lives in a secluded place, eats less, controls body, is free from false ego, anger, and hatred, is fully detached and renounced, and is in meditation (*dhyana yoga*) always, is the one elevated to the position of self-realisation. Thus transcendentally situated, one realises the Supreme *Brahmman* and enjoys eternal happiness. One can understand the ultimate truth only through devotional service, and by understanding this truth, one can merge with the Supreme. Though engaged in all kinds of activities, my pure devotee reaches eternal peace through my grace. In all activities, depend on me and be conscious of me always. You will be able to overcome all difficulties coming in your way. If you disobey this and act under false ego, you will be lost. If, out of false ego (*ahankar*), you decide not to fight, you are ignoring your prescribed duty and going in the wrong direction. Under illusion, you may decline my directions. But compelled by your own necessity, you may have to carry out your duty.

God is seated in the heart of every living being and is directing all activities of the material body. Surrender unto him and, through his grace, attain transcendental peace. Thus, I have explained to you knowledge still more confidential. After fully deliberating on what I said, do what you wish to do. Because you are my friend, I am imparting to you the most confidential of all knowledge, and that is for your benefit. Abandon all varieties of religion (*dharma*) and surrender to God. He will deliver you from all sinful consequences of your work.

Those who are not engaged in devotional service and who disregard God will never attain this knowledge. One who explains these supreme secrets to devotees is sure to reach God in the end. No one will be dearer to me than such a person. A person who studies this conversation between us is the enlightened person (*jnani*). One who listens with faith and without questioning becomes free from sinful reactions and reaches a happier level than others.

Have you heard this with an attentive mind? Are your ignorance and illusion now dispelled?

Arjuna:

Yes Vasudev. With your mercy, all my illusions have disappeared. I have regained my memory, I am free from doubt. I am now prepared to act according to your instructions.

(Sanjay, who with the spiritual power conferred on him by Veda Vyasa heard all that was said by Vasudev Krishna to Arjuna, was wonderstruck and concludes this part of his narration to Dhritharashtra with the words 'wherever there is an adviser like Krishna and an archer like Arjuna there will always be opulence, victory and morality'.)

West Asia: A Simmering Cauldron

West Asia is in the limelight once again. The propaganda blitz unleashed by corporate-controlled media is making it difficult for anyone to have a clear idea of what is actually happening there. The only thing one can see through TV channels is Israeli attacks on Gaza Strip, causing destruction of property and large-scale civilian casualties.

Israel's explanation for the latest attack is that the 'terrorist' organisation Hamas committed 'unprovoked' aggression against Israel which led to loss of life besides Israeli citizens being taken captive by the terrorists. This, therefore, is a retaliatory measure, and Gaza has been targeted because it happens to be the hideout of these terrorists. The attack is expected to continue 'till the terrorists are flushed out and Israeli citizens liberated from captivity'.

The United States, Canada, Britain and France lost no time in expressing solidarity with Israel. We have not heard anything from the Arab side. Perhaps that is not important for the media.

This is not an isolated incident. We are quite familiar with such incidents in the past. In fact, the whole of West Asia has been like an active volcano since the beginning of the twentieth century with its epicentre in Palestine. Ordinary people who have no idea of the past are naturally confused and are unable to have a coherent opinion on the issue. To have a clear idea, we have to dig deep into the past.

Before the First World War

Israel is the other name of Jacob, son of Isaac and grandson of Abraham. Jews consider themselves as the descendants of Abraham through Isaac and Jacob. The Jewish State carved out in West Asia in the twentieth century goes by the name 'Israel'.

Hebrew-speaking people who migrated and settled in Palestine (known as Canaan in ancient times) during their tribal stage evolved into Jews and Samaritans, Jews occupying the region of Judaea and Galilee, and Samaritans occupying Samaria.

According to Jewish tradition, Isaac inherited Canaan as a 'gift' from God (land 'promised' to Abraham by God). Following a famine in that region, Isaac's son and successor, Jacob migrated to Egypt with his wives and children. His descendants were enslaved by the Pharaohs of Egypt. Four hundred years later, Moses liberated the enslaved Jews and returned to the 'Promised Land'. Joshua, successor to Moses, conquered Canaan around the 15th century BC, and from that time began the organised existence of Jews in that region with the *Ten Commandments* (supposed to have been given to Moses by God on Mount Sinai) as the basis of their religious and social life. By about the 9th century BC, Jewish settlements in this region grouped themselves under two small kingdoms, Israel in the north and Judaea in the south.

Around the year 720 BC, Israel was invaded by the Assyrians, and the Jewish kingdom was destroyed. A large number of people belonging to this region were 'relocated' by the conquerors while the rest escaped to Judaea. Those who were relocated lost their identity and are mentioned in Jewish scriptures as the 'ten lost tribes'.

The Kingdom of Judaea survived for another 130 years. Around the year 586 BC, the Assyrian chieftain Nebuchadnezzar invaded Judaea and destroyed the kingdom. Large number of Jews were deported to Babylon and held in captivity.

The Achaemenid ruler Cyrus of Persia conquered the Babylonian kingdom around the year 539 BC and brought Babylonia and the Jewish settlements of Israel and Judaea under Persian control. He allowed the Jews held captive in Babylon to return to Judaea. Persian control over Jewish territory lasted for about 200 years. Alexander of Macedon invaded Persia and defeated the Achaemenid ruler Darius in 331 BC. Persian Empire collapsed, and in its place came the Greek Empire. Jewish territory came under Greek rule since then.

After Alexander's death in 323 BC, his empire was divided between his generals, Ptolemy taking the Egyptian region and Seleucus Nicator taking the Persian region. Greek dominance lasted for about 400 years, and, during this period, the Jews survived as a community without any political power, the southern region (Judaea) under Ptolemaic influence and the northern region (Samaria) under Seleucid influence.

During the 1st century AD, Romans began their eastern conquest. Within about 100 years, they succeeded in driving out the Greeks from this region, and Jewish regions under Greek rule came under the control of Rome.

Roman rule that followed was oppressive, and the Jews in Judaea and Samaria rose in revolt against the Romans. The rebellion assumed serious proportion and led to three major confrontations. In all these engagements, the Jews lost, and in the last battle (136 AD), Romans wiped out Jewish resistance.

Many Jews lost their lives, many were taken prisoner and sold in slave markets, and many escaped to neighbouring territories. Those who left their homeland migrated and spread to Europe, Africa and Asia during earlier days and to America after the discovery of that continent in the fifteenth-sixteenth century to live as refugees.

Wherever they settled, they organised themselves as small communities bonded by their social and religious identity. For livelihood, they made use of the opportunities available to them in the land of their settlement. To keep up their religious identity, 'Rabbinic Judaism' became helpful to them. This brand of Judaism was a modification of the earlier practice of temple-centred worship. It was started by Jews during their Babylonian exile days (sixth century BC). After the destruction of Jehovah's Temple at Jerusalem and the expulsion of Jews from Judaea towards the end of the first century AD, it became the only way to continue their faith. Temple rituals were replaced with prayer services in synagogues (places of worship). Rabbis (priests) managed the affairs of synagogues. No central organisation like the Church of Rome was there to oversee religious practices of the Jewish Diaspora.

For nearly 1800 years, Jews remained scattered all over the world with faint memories of their 'glorious' past made out through their religious literature. They never integrated with the people of the countries where they settled, and their hosts looked upon them as outsiders. Most of them picked up trading activity for livelihood and became notorious as money lenders and usurers, particularly in Russia and European countries. Shakespeare's Shylock in *The Merchant of Venice* is the caricature of a typical Jew of the Middle Ages. Christians hated them as they were considered primarily responsible for the crucifixion of Jesus.

Anti-Semitism (prejudice towards or discrimination against Jews) continued in Europe and Russia and reached its climax during the nineteenth century. The famous Dreyfus case (*L'Affair Dreyfus*) was an example. Alfred Dreyfus, a French army officer of Jewish descent, was falsely implicated in an espionage case and sentenced to life imprisonment by a French military court. Following the French military custom of those days, he was formally degraded by having the rank insignia, buttons and braid cut from his uniform and publicly paraded in the courtyard of *Ecole Militaire*. The real culprit, a French officer who passed on military secrets to Germans, was identified later, but the evidence was suppressed, and the court which tried him found him 'not guilty'.

Among those who witnessed the degrading and parading of Dreyfus was the Austro-Hungarian Jewish Journalist Theodor Herzl (1860-1904). This incident, together with the cry 'death to the Jews' heard from those who gathered to watch the parade, sent Herzl into a reflective mood. The enterprising and well-to-do Jewish community had been pushed into a marginalised existence in the land of their settlement. Anti-Jewish sentiment would make Jewish assimilation (integration into the surrounding culture) impossible, and the only solution to the Jewish problem, according to him, was to have a Jewish State. In 1896, he published a pamphlet under the name *Der Judenstaat* in which he elaborated his vision of a Jewish homeland. His ideas attracted international attention and became the basis of the Zionist movement which began towards the close of the nineteenth century.

The term Zionism is derived from Zion, a hill in Jerusalem which, according to Jewish tradition, housed the citadel of David (the legendary chieftain who ruled Israel and Judaea during the tenth century BC). 'Return to Zion' came into use from the time Jews held in captivity by the Babylonians were allowed to return to Judaea by the Persian King Cyrus. It symbolised the return to their 'homeland'. Zionism meant the desire of Jews stranded outside to return to their homeland, 'Eretz Israel' (the land of Israel according to Biblical tradition). The Zionist movement represented this desire.

Herzl made it a political movement and established the Zionist Congress in 1897. Its first session was held in Basel (Switzerland) the same year. Its goal was to build the infrastructure to further the cause of Jewish settlement in the homeland to be established.

Before we go ahead with the progress of this movement, we need to examine the developments in the West Asian region after the Jewish exodus to get an idea of the covert and overt influences those developments exercised on the course of this movement.

After the suppression of Jewish revolts and expulsion of Jews from their homeland, Romans reconstituted the Jewish territories of Judaea, Samaria, and Idumea into a Roman province under the name 'Syria Palaestina'. They also converted Jerusalem into a Greco-Roman city and repopulated the region vacated by the Jews with legionary veterans and Greco-Syrians from the surrounding regions. Very few Jews were left, and they continued in the Galilee region as an insignificant minority.

The Roman Emperor Constantine (280-337 AD), after his conversion to Christianity in the early fourth century, began to

Christianise the Roman Empire. As a result of his efforts, the province of Syria Palaestina came under Christian influence. Large number of Christian churches sprang up in this region, and places like Jerusalem and Bethlehem became Christian pilgrimage centres.

By the fifth century, western part of the Roman Empire crumbled. Eastern part continued as the Eastern Roman Empire or the Byzantine Empire with Constantinople as the seat of power. During Byzantine rule, there were occasional disturbances in the Syria Palaestina region due to revolts organised by different religious groups. The Sassanid ruler of Persia, Khosrow II, invaded and captured Jerusalem in 611. Although the lost territory was retaken seventeen years later, such loss of territory was indicative of the growing weakness of the Byzantine Empire.

After the successful unification of Arabian Peninsula under Islam by the first Caliph, Abu Bakr (632–634), Arab Muslims began their conquest and expansion in the West Asian region commencing their operations in southern and south-eastern Syria. The conquest which Abu Bakr began was continued after his death (634) by his successor, Caliph Omar (634–644). The Byzantine ruler resisted the Muslim advance but could not stop it. By 640, all of Palestine and Syria came under Muslim control.

Under the Umayyads (a Muslim dynasty that gained power in 661 from the Meccans and Madinans who led the Islamic community initially), Palestine together with Syria formed an important province of the Muslim territory. The Umayyad Caliph Omar II (717-720) imposed humiliating restrictions on non-Muslim subjects, particularly the Christians. Conversions arising from convenience as well as conviction increased. Together with conversion was the steady inflow of tribals from the desert. This changed the religious character of the Palestinians. The predominantly Christian population gradually became predominantly Arabic-speaking Muslims.

Umayyad Caliphate ended in 750, and in its place came the Abbasid Caliphate based in Baghdad. The process of Islamisation gained momentum during the Abbasid rule. Abbasid Caliphs encouraged the settlement and fortification of coastal Palestine to secure it against Byzantine attack. The Caliphate shifted from Baghdad to Cairo (Egypt) with the rise of the Fatimid dynasty in the tenth century. The Fatimid Caliph al-Hakim (996-1021) ordered the destruction of Christian churches in Palestine and tightened restrictions on non-Muslim population.

When the Caliphate forces advanced to Eastern Europe, Christian nations of Europe organised the 'Crusades' against Islam with the blessings of the Pope. Between 1095 and 1291, there were numerous expeditions, and the Crusaders initially enjoyed some success in the Palestinian region. Jerusalem fell to the Christians. But in the end, Arabs recaptured the territories lost and repulsed European forces from the West Asian region.

With that, a turbulent chapter in the history of Palestine came to an end. The Mamluks (the slave dynasty that originated during the Abbasid Caliphate) ruled the Palestine region, with brief interruptions, for the next 600 years. Muslims constituted the majority, and Islam became the dominant religion of this region.

Byzantine Empire collapsed after the Ottoman Sultan Mehmed II captured Constantinople in 1453. The term 'Ottoman' is a dynastic appellation derived from Osman (Uthman in Arabic) who founded the dynasty and laid the foundation for the empire known as 'Ottoman Empire' about the year 1300 with Constantinople (later, Istanbul) as the seat of power. His ancestors were nomadic tribals who originated in Central Asia and moved into Anatolia during their migrant stage. These tribals became Turkish warriors known as Ghazis after their conversion to Islam, and they emerged as a political power in Turkey (Anatolia) during the 14th century. Defeating other contestants, they extended the empire to cover the Middle East, Turkey and Eastern Europe during the fifteenth and sixteenth centuries. In 1516, the Ottoman Sultan Selim I defeated the Mamluks and brought Palestine under Ottoman rule.

Between the Two World Wars

The First World War (1914-18) was a turning point for Palestine. Ottoman Empire entered the war as an ally of Germany and had to suffer defeat and dismemberment at the end of the war. Its possessions in West Asia and Europe were lost. In 1917, British forces entered Palestine, and by 1918, the region came under British control. In the Sykes-Picot Agreement of 1916 between Britain and France, it was envisioned that Palestine would be made an international territory in the event of Ottoman defeat in the war. However, after the war, Palestine was left under British military occupation till 1920. A civil administration was established thereafter in anticipation of a formal League of Nations 'mandate' for Britain to rule it as a 'mandated territory'. The mandate given by the League came into effect in 1923.

We now continue with the progress of the Zionist movement from where we left it. To ensure Jewish support for the war, particularly that of the wealthy Jewish lobby in the United States, the British Government formulated a plan for the fulfilment of the Jewish desire for a homeland. British foreign secretary Arthur

Balfour conveyed the British Government's support for a Jewish 'national home' in Palestine to the Zionist Federation through a formal letter in 1917. It came to be known as the 'Balfour Declaration'. The exact wording of the Declaration is as given below:

'His Majesty's Government view with favour the establishment in Palestine of a national home for the Jewish people and will use their best endeavours to facilitate the achievement of this object, it being clearly understood that nothing shall be done which may prejudice the civil and religious rights of existing non-Jewish communities in Palestine, or the rights and political status enjoyed by the Jews in any other country'.

British occupation of Palestine and mandate given by the League of Nations created favourable conditions for implementation of the promises contained in the Balfour Declaration. Between 1919 and 1923, about forty thousand Jews, mainly from Eastern Europe, migrated to Palestine. Many of the Jewish immigrants were ideologically driven pioneers trained in agriculture and were capable of establishing self-sustaining economies. They developed the Jezreel Valley and Hefer Plain marshes in northern Palestine to make them suitable for agriculture. This was followed by the creation of a labour federation, an elected assembly, a council for administration and the *Haganah*, forerunner of the Israeli Defence Forces. Their effort was funded and supported by Zionist organisations.

Between 1924 and 1929, about eighty-two thousand more Jews arrived as a result of increased anti-Semitism in Europe. The vast majority of these immigrants were middle-class people belonging mainly to Poland, Romania and Lithuania, and they moved into the growing townships establishing small businesses and light industries.

Anti-Jewish policy followed by Hitler led to mass migration of Jews from Germany, Poland, Austria, and Czechoslovakia. A new wave of two lakh fifty thousand emigrants arrived in Palestine during the period 1933-36. British efforts to impose restrictions on immigration only led to clandestine immigration. The new emigrants contained large number of professionals, doctors, lawyers and professors. Jewish population in Palestine reached 450,000 by 1940.

Conflicts erupted between Jewish settlers and local Palestinian people as emigration gained momentum. Both fought for survival. For the local people (mainly Arabs), it was eviction from the land which was under their control for over 1300 years; for the Jews, establishing new homes in a hostile environment. In the beginning, it was a clash over land, habitat, water and religious rights. Later, it developed into a conflict of 'national identity', and became brutal, organised uprisings.

A major Arab riot against Jews took place in 1929, and it led to many deaths and depopulation of the Jewish settlement in Hebron. This was followed by more violence during the uprising of 1936-39. Sensing that the situation was going out of control, Britain brought out a White Paper in 1939 severely restricting immigration to seventy-five thousand people for the next five years. That only led to more illegal immigration.

For the rest of West Asia too, the period was quite crucial. To ensure Arab support for the war against the Ottoman Empire, Britain came out with a promise of total independence to Arabs after the war. Taking this promise in good faith, Hussein bin Ali al-Hashimi, Sharif and Emir of Mecca, agreed to offer support to Britain and organised the Arab revolt against Ottomans. That was of immense help to the British. But Britain had already made a secret agreement with France (The Sykes-Picots Agreement) in 1916 to partition Ottoman territory in West Asia between them in the event of Ottoman defeat in the war.

Hoping that Britain would honour the promise given to Sharif Hussein, Hussein's third son Emir Faisal who led the Arab revolt entered Damascus in 1918 along with General Allenby, commander of the British forces, and established the post-war government in Syria. Arabs believed that Damascus would become the seat of power for the independent Arab State promised by Britain. The Syrian National Conference convened in 1919, attended by representatives from all parts of Greater Syria including Palestine and Lebanon, adopted a resolution in 1920 declaring independence for Syria and proclaiming Faisal as the King of all Arabs.

When French forces landed in Beirut demanding implementation of the Sykes-Picots Agreement, British forces withdrew from Damascus, leaving the Arabs to face the French. The Sykes-Picots Agreement provided for French takeover of the northern part of Ottoman territory (Syria and Lebanon) and British takeover of the southern part (Palestine, Jordan, and Iraq). This arrangement was formalised through the League of Nations mandate in 1920 with the modification that Jerusalem, Bethlehem and surrounding areas should be under international governance.

Arabs felt cheated by Britain and refused to accept the League mandate. The newly formed Government of Syria began conscription and preparation for war. But they were unequal to the better-trained and better-equipped French, and, in the battle that ensued, they lost. Emir Faisal was expelled from Syria. French forces entered Damascus and established a mandatory regime over Syria and Lebanon. Lebanon separated from Syria in 1926. Syria and Lebanon became independent nations after the mandatory rule ended in 1946.

When French forces captured Damascus and expelled Emir Faisal in 1920, Faisal's elder brother, Emir Abdullah, moved his forces from the Arab kingdom of Hejaz to Jordan with a view to liberating Damascus from French control. Britain dissuaded him on the ground that he had no chance of victory over the French. He was convinced and made no further move with his plan. Meanwhile, the Iraqi conference convened by Arab chieftains invited him to take over the Kingdom of Iraq. He refused and established his emirate in Jordan with the acceptance of Jordanian people. Britain accommodated him as the King of Jordan under the League mandate, and, when the mandate ended in 1946, he became King of independent Jordan.

At the close of the First World War, Britain was in possession of the three Ottoman provinces that made up modern Iraq – Basra, Mosul and Bagdad. Each of these provinces possessed its own separate ethnic, cultural and religious identity. Basra was linked to Persia through trade and history. Bagdad looked to Palestine and Damascus for trade and cultural influences. People of Mosul were not Arabs but Kurds of Euro-Persian descent. In 1918, the two provinces, Basra and Bagdad, were united and brought under one administration. Under the League of Nations mandate of 1920, Britain became the *de facto* ruler of Mesopotamia and Mosul. The mandate provided for semi-autonomous status for Kurdish areas. Britain complied with this requirement initially, but later on, those areas were integrated with the other two provinces to form the Kingdom of Iraq.

Vast majority of people of the newly carved out kingdom had never been exposed to a central government rule and were dependent on tribal chiefs for basic administration. Also, majority of them were illiterate with very little exposure to law and order. Because of the difficulty of uniting these diverse people and carrying on the administration, British administration relied on local chieftains to govern them on its behalf.

When the League mandate came into effect, Arabs and Kurds refused to accept it, and organised demonstrations calling for British withdrawal from Mesopotamia. When they found that the British were not in a relenting mood, demonstrations developed into open revolt. British administration had to struggle for three months to suppress the revolt and restore law and order.

The rebellion convinced Britain that it would be difficult to carry on in Iraq unless the mandatory rule was replaced by an administration acceptable to the people. In the Cairo conference of 1921, it was decided that a single leader who could be manipulated to serve British interests and, at the same time, be acceptable to the Arabs would be the best arrangement. Emir Faisal who was expelled from Syria was considered the most suitable candidate because, being a descendant of the Prophet, he would be acceptable to most Muslims, and, knowing that he would be dependent on British support for the retention of his throne, he would be a manageable tool for preserving British interests. Faisal was brought and crowned King of Iraq in 1921.

The mandate was replaced by a treaty to give an impression that the British were in Iraq not as rulers but as equal partners and well-wishers. It retained most provisions of the mandate in an 'advisory' form to ensure that British control remained as before. The League mandate ended in 1932, and Iraq became independent from that time.

An important outcome of Anglo-French mandatory rule over West Asian region was the strengthening of Arab nationalism which originated during the early years of the twentieth century.

The rich heritage of Arabic language, memory of centuries of Arab cultural predominance in the Mediterranean World, and the religious bond based on Islam provided a common historical tradition which contributed to the feeling of oneness among the Arabs. This was nourished by Ottoman domination over them lasting for over four centuries. Rise of European nationalism at the end of the Middle Ages and liberation of the Slavic minorities of the Balkan region from Ottoman domination in the nineteenth century provided inspiration to the Arab *elite* in important cities like Damascus and Bagdad to think in terms of a similar Arab movement for political unity based on nationalist aspirations.

In 1911, Arab intellectuals and politicians from West Asia formed an organisation called *al-Fatat* (The Young Arab Society) in Paris. Its stated aim was 'raising the level of the Arab nation to the level of modern nations'. In the first few years of its existence, *al-Fatat* called only for greater autonomy within the Ottoman Empire, not independence. For the Imperial Ottomans, even such an idea was repugnant, and they cracked down on the organisation. That led to the organisation going underground and hardening its attitude. Call for autonomy changed to demand for independence.

Growing Arab nationalism appeared a useful weapon for the British in their war against the Ottomans during the First World War. Sharif Hussein of Mecca was approached for support, and he was promised Arab independence after the war in return for his support. Taking this promise in good faith, Hussein organised the Arab revolt against the Ottomans. With the Ottoman defeat and withdrawal from West Asia, the Arabs felt that they would be able to form a united Arab nation in the area vacated by the Ottomans with Sharif Hussein as its leader.

Emir Faisal, son of Sharif Hussein, who led the Arab revolt entered Damascus in 1918, and the Syrian National Conference proclaimed him King of all Arabs in 1920. By this time, along with many Arab intellectuals and military officers of West Asia, Faisal had joined the *al-Fatat*. Following this proclamation, Damascus became the co-coordinating centre for the Arab nationalist movement, while Jerusalem, Beirut and Bagdad became important support bases.

When leaders of this movement came to know of the Sykes-Picot Agreement and Balfour Declaration, they felt cheated by Britain. They realised that Arabs were not going to be free after the war but would become subjects of the two colonial powers, Britain and France. The tag 'mandatory rule' could not conceal its true intention. What was more, the British idea of a 'national home' for Jews in Palestine was like adding insult to injury. Anti-foreign sentiment, as in the case of other colonial countries of Asia and Africa, became the backbone of the Arab nationalist movement since then.

Arab nationalism gave birth to what came to be known as 'pan-Arabism', an ideology that espoused the unification of all Arab people in a single nation-state comprising Arab countries of West Asia and North Africa from the Atlantic Ocean to the Arabian Sea. Most of these countries were under colonial rule and had anti-foreign sentiment as a common binding factor in addition to religion and language. It gained momentum as western domination over this region became more pronounced in the days that followed. Formation of the State of Israel in 1948 brought them closer together to form a united front against Israel.

After the Second World War

West Asia moved rapidly to become a simmering cauldron during the period that followed the Second World War.

The mandatory system established by the League of Nations came to an end in West Asia after the war, and the Arab countries which became independent were admitted as members of the United Nations. That gave an impression that West Asia became free from outside interference.

But that was an illusion. Britain and France had built up huge assets in West Asia during their colonial domination. Suez Canal, constructed in the latter half of the nineteenth century, became strategically important for Britain and France as it controlled the line of communication with their Asian colonies. They bought maximum number of shares in the Suez Canal Company and controlled its management. Petroleum resources of the Persian Gulf region constituted another attraction for colonial powers. According to published data on oil and natural gas resources, West Asia holds about 51% of the total global reserves. Ever since the discovery of petroleum deposits in this region in the early part of the twentieth century, industrially advancing nations of the west were exploiting this source and making huge profits. Protection of these economic and strategic interests was of paramount significance to Britain and France, and they had to institute measures to ensure the safety of their assets. And that would virtually paralyse the independence of Arab nations.

Britain's 'magnanimity' towards the Jews pushed the Palestinian Arabs into a life and death struggle during the years that followed the war. Jewish immigration continued in spite of

British restrictions, and it was facilitated by *Mossad Le'aliyabet*, a branch of the para-military organisation *Haganah*. About one lakh ten thousand Jews entered Palestine illegally during this period, and they included many Holocaust survivors from German-occupied areas.

With the creation of the United Nations after the war, the League of Nations lapsed, and Britain announced in 1947 its decision to terminate the Palestine mandate. Responsibility to decide the future of Palestine was left to the United Nations.

The United Nations formed a special committee to go into the question and suggest a plan for the future of Palestine. The committee submitted its report in May 1947, recommending the division of Palestine into an Arab State and a Jewish State. The proposed Arab State would include western part of Galilee, hilly country of Samaria and Judaea and Gaza Strip with a section of the desert along the Egyptian border. The proposed Jewish State would include eastern Galilee, the coastal plain stretching from Haifa to Rehovot and most of the Negev desert. A separate enclave was to be formed encompassing Jerusalem, Bethlehem and surrounding areas, and it was to be brought under international governance. According to this plan, Jews who constituted 33% of the population in 1946 would get 56% of the land while Arabs, in spite of their numerical superiority, should be satisfied with the remaining 44%. Naturally, the Arabs opposed this partition plan while the Jews welcomed it.

The resolution introduced in the UN General Assembly in November 1947 to implement these proposals was put to vote and passed with a two-third majority, but it could not be implemented in the face of Arab opposition.

British mandate on Palestine came to an end in 1948. On 14 May 1948, the day before British withdrawal, Jewish leaders declared the independent state of Israel. Soon after the British withdrawal, war erupted between the newly established Israeli state and neighbouring Arab countries. Egypt, Jordan, Syria, Iraq, Saudi Arabia and Yemen sent their expeditionary forces to Palestine. The Arab invasion was denounced by the United States, the Soviet Union and the UN Secretary-General. The United States and European countries, in general, were sympathetic to the Jews and supplied equipment and military hardware to them. Support for the Arabs came from a few Asian and African states only.

The war, which commenced in May 1948, lasted for about nine months. It ended with the signing of armistice agreements in 1949 by the fighting forces. As a result of this war, Israel controlled the area proposed by the United Nations for the Jewish State and about 60% of the area proposed for the Arab State. Israel took control of west Jerusalem, which was meant to be part of the international zone. Jordan took control of East Jerusalem and the territory on the west of the Jordan River which came to be known as the 'West Bank'. Egypt occupied 'Gaza Strip'. The United Nations appointed a truce supervision organisation to monitor ceasefire violations and forcible alteration of the line of control agreed to in the armistice agreements.

The conflict triggered a significant demographic change in West Asia. About seven lakh fifty thousand Palestinian Arabs fled or were expelled from their homes in the area that came under Israeli control, and they became refugees in neighbouring countries. Almost equal number of Jews moved to Israel during the three years following the war of which about one-third was from neighbouring countries.

Immediately after the declaration of the independent State of Israel, Jewish leaders formed a Provisional Government for the State of Israel. It was promptly given *de facto* recognition by the United States. The Soviet Union gave *de jure* recognition. *De facto* recognition given by the United States was converted to *de jure* recognition in January 1949. On the basis of a majority decision, Israel was admitted as a member state of the United Nations in May 1949.

A new chapter opened up in West Asian politics with the appearance of the United States on the scene. 'The Cold War' and 'oil interests' were primarily responsible for the American entry.

'Cold War' was the term used to denote the geo-political tension between the United States and the Soviet Union that developed after the Second World War. The two superpowers avoided a major conflict between them but supported regional conflicts in the form of 'proxy wars', and that was the reason for prefixing the word 'cold' with the word 'war'. West Asia got involved in the Cold War as a result of the contest between the superpowers to fill in the political vacuum created by the French and British withdrawal from the region.

Ever since anti-foreign sentiment became the rallying point for Arab nationalism, hatred for the west made Arabs lean more and more towards the Soviet Union, politically at least, if not ideologically. The Soviet Union, although it recognised Israel when it was formed, began extending sympathy and support to the Arab cause as part of its Cold War strategy. For the United States, preventing Soviet influence in West Asia was an essential part of its policy of 'containment of communism'.

The United States is responsible for 25% of the world's oil consumption while having only 3% of the world's proven oil reserves. That makes the country dependent on imports, and Gulf region is the major supplier. With the withdrawal of Britain and France from West Asia, control over the oil-producing region became a necessity to protect the interests of foreign companies working in this region as also to ensure uninterrupted supply and price stability.

Visible political control was one important factor that nourished nationalist movements in colonies. Knowing this, the United States avoided this method and tried to establish its hold through pliant regimes. Helping feudal chieftains or ambitious military men to assume power and establish autocratic rule in the states carved out by Britain and France during their mandatory rule and sustaining the Jewish State in Palestine with military and financial help were the methods adopted to keep West Asia under control. These 'leaders' and the State of Israel, dependent on the United States for their survival, could be relied on to protect American interests in the region.

For the people of West Asia, that meant a frustrating and turbulent period ahead in their onward movement. Frequent regime changes engineered by the United States, direct American aggression, interstate wars, political assassinations and Israeli-Arab confrontations would destroy political stability and peace in this region.

The first civilian government formed in Syria after it became independent in 1946 was overthrown by the Syrian army chief in 1949 with the active support of the United States. Once in power, the chief made several decisions that benefitted the

United States. Two unsuccessful attempts were made during the 1956-57 period to topple the 'left-leaning' Syrian Government and replace it with a 'pro-American' Government. A well-planned attempt to assassinate the Army chief, head of military intelligence and the leader of the Syrian Communist Party in 1957 had to be aborted because of leakage of the plan before implementation. The American intelligence agency was behind all these conspiracies.

In 1958, Gamal Abdal Nasser of Egypt and Shukri al-Kuwatli of Syria jointly announced the merger of the two countries, creating the United Arab Republic as a preliminary to the establishment of the unified Arab State in West Asia. The union was not a success. Following a military coup in 1961, successfully carried out with American assistance, Syria seceded from the union and re-established itself as the Syrian Arab Republic. Instability in that country characterised the next eighteen months with various *coups* culminating in the establishment of the National Council of the Revolutionary Command to take over the legislative and executive authority in 1963. This takeover was engineered by the Ba'ath Party.

The Ba'ath Party was formed in Syria in 1947 with an ideology mixing Arab nationalism, pan-Arabism, anti-imperialism and socialism. It grew fast and established its branches in other Arab countries. By 1954, it had become the second largest party in Syria. Pan-Arabism or uniting all Arabs to form one state extending from the Atlantic Ocean to the Arabian Sea was its declared objective. Although the term socialism decorated its title, the party was totally anti-communist. Its anti-communist credentials enabled it to become a beneficiary of American assistance.

In 1970, Hafez al-Assad effected a 'bloodless' *coup* and took over power in Syria ousting the civilian party leadership. His rule lasted till the year 2000.

British mandate over Jordan ended in 1946, and Abdullah continued as King of independent Jordan. He upheld his alliance with the British and, when Britain withdrew from the region, switched over his loyalty to the Americans. That was against the Arab sentiment, but for him, his position was more important than Arab sentiment. During the Arab-Israeli conflict of 1948, Jordan annexed the West Bank. That angered Arab countries like Saudi Arabia, Egypt and Syria which were all for the creation of the Palestinian State of which the West Bank would be a part. Abdullah was assassinated in 1951 and was succeeded by his son Talal, who ruled Iraq till his abdication in 1952. Talal's son Hussein who was crowned King in 1952 after his father's abdication ruled till his death in 1999. The policy of cooperation with western powers initiated by Abdullah was followed by his successors also. For their cooperation, Jordan was handsomely rewarded with financial assistance worth fourteen billion US dollars since 1952.

British mandate over Iraq ended in 1932, and Iraq became an independent nation from that time. Emir Faisal who was crowned King in 1921 continued as King till his death in 1933. He was succeeded by his son Ghazi, and, on Ghazi's death in 1939, Ghazi's son Faisal was crowned as King Faisal II.

In 1927, huge petroleum deposits were detected in the Kirkuk region of Iraq. Exploration rights of these oil fields were given to a British firm with the name 'Iraqi Petroleum Company'. This company, jointly owned by some of the world's largest oil companies, established a virtual monopoly on exploration and production of petroleum products in Iraq till 1961. In 1956, Iraq was made to join the Central Treaty Organisation (CENTO), an anti-Soviet alliance sponsored by the United States.

In 1958, Iraq tried to bring about a union between Iraq and Jordan under Hashemite rule and invited Kuwait to become a partner in the proposed union. This was to counter the move initiated by Gamal Abdal Nasser of Egypt to unite Egypt and Syria in the name of pan-Arabism. Angered by this move, Nasser launched a media campaign challenging the legitimacy of the Iraqi monarchy. Inspired by Nasser's outpourings, officers of the Iraqi Army led by Brigadier Abd al-Karim Qasim rose in revolt, overthrew Faisal's Government and assassinated Faisal along with his Prime Minister Nuri as-Said. The government formed by Qasim proclaimed Iraq a republic, rejected the idea of union with Jordan and distanced itself from the American-sponsored CENTO. He also began to curb the Iraqi Petroleum Company's monopoly by restricting its operations.

Qasim's Government was overthrown in 1963 in a *coup* led by General Ahmed Hasan al-Bakr and Colonel Abdul Salam Arif. Qasim was a left-leaning nationalist, while Hasan al-Bakr and Colonel Arif were Ba'athists.

In spite of power struggles and changes at the top level, the Ba'ath Party remained in power after the 1963 coup. During Ba'athist rule, Iraq registered some economic progress, particularly after nationalisation of the Iraqi Petroleum Company in 1972.

Following al-Bakr's resignation in 1979, Saddam Hussein became the President of Iraq. During his tenure as President, Iraq was drawn into wars with Iran, Kuwait and a coalition led by the United States. War with Iran commenced in 1980 and lasted for eight years. War with Kuwait began in August 1990 and merged with the coalition-led Gulf War which ended in February 1991. Iraq was ruined by these wars. Saddam continued till the United States invaded again and captured him in 2003. He was tried on trumped-up charges and executed.

The latter half of the twentieth century witnessed a series of conflicts between Israel and its neighbouring Arab states. The first confrontation occurred when Gamal Abdel Nasser of Egypt nationalised the Suez Canal Company in 1956. Britain and France planned an attack on Egypt with the intention of taking over the company. They advised Israel to invade Egypt, and the plan was to take the Israeli invasion as a pretext for armed intervention in the name of protecting the Canal. In compliance, Israel invaded Egypt and, at the early stages of the war, made territorial gains in Gaza Strip and Sinai Peninsula. But they had to be given up when the United Nations intervened and brought the war to an end. The only gain was the right of passage for Israel through the Gulf of Aqaba.

The Six-Day War of 1967 was the next. Within ten years of the Suez crisis, Israel was again at war with the Arabs, this time a coalition of Arab states (primarily Egypt, Syria and Jordan). In May 1967, President Nasser announced the cancellation of Israel's right of passage through the Gulf of Aqaba and ordered withdrawal of the United Nations Emergency Force deployed on the Egypt-Israel border. Israel retaliated with airstrikes destroying Egyptian airfields and ground attacks on Sinai and Gaza Strip. Egyptian forces resisted but could not stop the Israeli advance. Jordan and Syria joined hands with Egypt shortly thereafter, launching their ground attacks from the eastern and northern regions respectively. But they also failed in their attempt to halt the Israeli move.

By the sixth day of the conflict, Israel captured the whole of Sinai Peninsula and Gaza Strip (occupied by Egypt in 1949), Syria's Golan Heights and the West Bank (including East Jerusalem, occupied by Jordan in 1949). The hostility ended with the signing of a ceasefire agreement. About three lakh Palestinians and one lakh Syrians fled or were expelled from the West Bank and Golan Heights, and they became refugees in neighbouring countries.

Israel celebrated its victory. For the western nations also, it was an occasion to rejoice because it was a triumph for them too in their effort to prevent the growth and consolidation of Arab nationalism which was threatening their vested interests.

The Arab League, an organisation founded in 1945 to build Arab unity, decided not to recognise Israel, not to have any negotiation with Israel and not to meekly accept peace brokered by western nations. The Palestinian Liberation Organisation (PLO), established in 1964, became more determined after the war in pursuing its declared objective of evicting Jews from Palestine. Defeat in the war convinced Arab leaders that it was difficult to defeat Israel in a regular war as Israel had the financial and military backing of the United States. Resistance to Israel thereafter began to take the shape of terrorist attacks and guerilla warfare.

Anti-west sentiment which was growing among the Arabs pushed them more and more towards a pro-Soviet stand in international relations. The Soviet Union reciprocated with military help and full support in the United Nations whenever the Palestine issue came up. Most countries in Asia and Africa also sympathised with the Arab cause, and those who did not recognise Israel till then became more determined to follow their non-recognition policy. Soviet bloc in Eastern Europe which established diplomatic relations with Israel broke off relations, and some of them even expelled Jews who remained within their territories.

Jewish emigration and settlement as also the planned economic development during the early days were sponsored by the State, and that gave an impression that Israel was following a 'socialist' programme. That could be a possible reason for the Soviet Union's sympathy at the early stage. When Israel began to lean more and more towards the west, the Soviet Union began to distance itself. It did not, however, break off diplomatic relations.

The ceasefire agreement was not followed by any peace treaty, and hostility soon broke out along the Suez Canal. It began with limited artillery duels and small-scale incursion into Sinai. But by 1969, it developed into full-scale operations with large-scale shelling along the Suez Canal, extensive aerial warfare and commando raids. Hostilities continued till 1970 and ended with a ceasefire agreement. The frontiers remained as before.

Within another three years, large-scale hostilities renewed. On 6 October 1973, Egypt and Syria jointly launched an attack, Egypt invading Sinai and Syria invading the Golan Heights (both under Israeli occupation since 1967). It came to be known as the 'Yom Kippur War' because the day of commencement of the war was a holy day for Jews (Day of Atonement or *Yom Kippur*). It lasted for eighteen days. Following the outbreak of hostilities, both the United States and the Soviet Union initiated massive supply efforts to their allies engaged in the war. That threatened to make the war a confrontation between the two nuclear-armed superpowers.

During the initial stage, Egypt and Syria made some gains, but after three days of heavy fighting, Israel succeeded in halting the Egyptian offensive in Sinai and pushing Syrians back to the pre-war ceasefire line on the Golan Heights. Israel then launched a counter-attack which put the coalition partners under great stress. Under the United Nations initiative, a ceasefire was arranged effective from 25 October 1973. While the Israeli-Egypt border remained peaceful, tension remained high on the Israel-Syria front. By March 1974, the situation became increasingly unstable. Again, under US initiative, a ceasefire was arranged between Israel and Syria, and it came into effect in May 1974.

Under pressure from the United States, King Hussein of Jordan refrained from participating in the war. Towards the end, however, he came forward in support of Syria, and historians interpret this move as a clever attempt to show that Jordan was also a participant in the war. He seems to have struck a secret deal with Israel for being left undisturbed in return for non-participation in the war.

The Yom Kippur War had far-reaching implications. Initial success in the war helped the Arabs to overcome the despondency caused by successive defeats in the earlier wars. Israel recognised that despite their impressive performance on the battlefield, there could be no guarantee for their ability to retain their military superiority over the Arabs forever. Backing of the war by the superpowers showed that West Asia could well be a starting point for a third World War.

In October 1973, Arab members of the Organisation of Petroleum Exporting Countries (OPEC) led by King Faisal of Saudi Arabia declared an embargo on the export of petroleum products to the United States and European countries which supported Israel. They also decided to reduce oil production. That created an energy crisis in western countries and, apart from forcing European countries to withdraw recognition of Israel, compelled the United States to follow an even-handed policy in West Asia.

Under United States initiative, Anwar Sadat of Egypt and Menachem Begin of Israel met in 1978 at Camp David in the United States to negotiate a permanent peace. Their talks led to the signing of a peace agreement (known as the 'Camp David Accords') in 1979. According to this agreement, Israel vacated Sinai (Egyptian territory occupied by Israel during the Six-Day War) in return for Egypt's recognition of Israel as a sovereign nation.

Jordan and Syria were not invited and had no part in this agreement. The whole Arab world was enraged by this agreement. Egypt, under President Nasser, was an icon of Arab nationalism. Anwar Sadat who succeeded Nasser in 1970 was pro-American, and his personal interests were more important to him than Arab nationalism. After the Yom Kippur War, he began to distance himself from the Soviet Union and strengthen relations with the United States. All these were considered as betrayal of Arab interests, and he was assassinated in 1981 by a member of the extremist organisation called 'al-Jihad'. Egypt was suspended from the Arab League for the unpardonable act of extending recognition to Israel.

Golan Heights forming part of Syrian territory, captured by Israel during the Six-Day War (1967), remained with Israel as an occupied territory. Although Syria tried to take it back during the Yom Kippur War (1973), it did not succeed. In 1981, Israeli Parliament (*Knesset*) enacted a law making Golan Heights an integral part of Israel. The international community refused to accept the unilateral action of Israel and continued to treat it as an occupied territory. However, the United States recognised Israeli sovereignty over Golan Heights in 2019. East Jerusalem, under occupation of Israel, was also recognised by the United States as Israeli territory.

In June 1982, Israel invaded Lebanon with the aim of driving out PLO forces conducting guerilla raids on Israel from southern Lebanon. PLO, operating with its base in Jordan after the 1967 war, relocated to Lebanon after it was driven out from Jordan by King Hussein in 1971, and was carrying out its activities from Lebanon since then. Israelis advanced into Lebanon and captured Beirut. As a result of this invasion, PLO forces had to move out from Lebanon and establish in Tunisia. Israel withdrew from Lebanon after a peace treaty was signed in May 1983. However, while withdrawing, a contingent of Israeli forces was left in South Lebanon to ensure that the area was not used for guerilla attacks against Israel.

Following the Israeli invasion, the Shia Islamist group in Lebanon formed a party named 'Hezbollah' (party of God) drawing inspiration from Iran. Its political wing was named 'Loyalty to the Resistance Block' and para-military wing went by the name 'Jihad Council'. Its declared aim was the expulsion of imperialist forces and their allies from Lebanon. The period from 1985 to 2000 witnessed protracted armed conflict between the Hezbollah and Israeli forces stationed in South Lebanon. That compelled Israel to withdraw completely from South Lebanon by the year 2000.

Growing resentment against Israeli military occupation of the West Bank and Gaza Strip reached its climax by 1987 and began to express itself as general strikes, economic boycotts and refusal to work in Israeli settlements besides sporadic violence. Israel deployed some eighty thousand soldiers in response, and resorted to inhuman methods while dealing with the 'offenders'. Corporate-controlled western media concealed Israel's human rights violations and tried to paint the Arabs as aggressors.

Under United States initiative, peace process began in 1993. Israel and the PLO signed what came to be known as the 'Oslo Accords I and II', the first one at Washington DC (US) in 1993 and the second one at Taba (Egypt) in 1995. It was a declaration of principles and was aimed at achieving a peace treaty based on UN Resolution of 1967 which stipulated Israeli withdrawal from occupied areas and fulfilling the right of Palestinian people to self-determination in return for PLO's recognition of Israel as a sovereign state and Israel's recognition of PLO as the representative of Palestinian people. A 'Palestinian National Authority (PNA)' was constituted to conduct limited self-governance in the West Bank and Gaza. The PLO which was given 'observer' status in the UN General Assembly in 1974 was to give up its earlier militant stand and relocate to the occupied territory.

The attempt to come to an understanding on the basis of the Oslo Accords met with resistance from Israeli and Palestinian extremists. Israeli Prime Minister Yitzhak Rabin who signed the Oslo Accords was assassinated in 1995. Binyamin Netanyahu who succeeded him was against the peace process. He did not take any interest in pursuing it and uncertainties continued.

The Oslo Accords provided that agreement should be reached on all issues between the two sides within a period of five years. However, the interim process put in place to move towards a settlement satisfied neither the Israeli nor the Palestinian side.

Another summit was held in Camp David in the year 2000 under American initiative to continue the peace effort, but this time no progress could be made for want of cooperation from either side. Failure of the summit triggered a major uprising by Palestinians against the Israeli occupation followed by a period of heightened violence between 2000 and 2005.

The Sharm el-Sheikh summit of 2005, attended by leaders of Israel, PLA, Egypt and Jordan, brought the uprising to an end. Both sides agreed to stop militant activities, and Israel agreed to withdraw troops from those parts of West Bank it had re-occupied while fighting Palestinian militants.

In September 2005, Israel pulled out from Gaza Strip. All Jewish settlers were evacuated from Gaza, and their homes were demolished. In the same way, military disengagement took place in northern part of West Bank the same year. Four Jewish settlements in this area were evacuated. However, Israel continued to maintain control over Gaza's air and maritime space, six of Gaza's seven land crossings, a no-go buffer zone within the territory and population registry. Gaza's dependence on Israel for its water supply, electricity, telecommunication and other utilities continued as before.

Because of this, Gaza Strip is still considered an occupied territory by the United Nations and international observers. Israel took the move to end ground control in these areas because of its calculation that if it became necessary to accept a Palestine state under the Oslo Accords or any other agreement in future, management of Gaza Strip and West Bank with their Arab majority would pose problems.

The PNA to which local administration was handed over as per provisions of the Oslo Accords conducted an election in

2006 in Palestinian territories to elect representatives for the Palestinian Legislative Council. The 'Hamas', a Sunni Islamist, anti-imperialist resistance movement founded in 1987, won the election in Gaza Strip defeating its rival, the secular Fatah Party which was holding power till then. In the West Bank, however, the Fatah managed to retain its control. Gaza Strip remained under the control of Hamas since then as no election was conducted thereafter. Hamas rejected all agreements signed with Israel and began to follow its declared confrontationist policy. As a result of this development, Israel had to face threats from two radical outfits, the Hezbollah in the north and the Hamas in the southwest. PLO which was considered as the representative of Palestinian people began to lose relevance because of its compromising attitude.

Islamic Republic of Iran, established after the overthrow of Iranian monarchy in 1979, became a close ally of the Arabs in their struggle against Israel. What began as covert support to the Shia-dominated Hezbollah in 1985 developed into a proxy war with Israel by 2005. By 2006, Iran became actively involved in supporting Hezbollah and, in parallel, began supporting Hamas and Palestinian Islamic Jihad, especially in Gaza Strip.

Backed by Iran, Hezbollah attacked Israel from Lebanon in July 2006. Israel responded with ground and air attacks. The war lasted for two months and concluded with a United Nations-sponsored ceasefire. Both Hezbollah and Israel withdrew their forces from Southern Lebanon.

Hamas which came to power in Gaza Strip after defeating the Fatah Party in the election held in 2006 clashed with the Fatah in 2007, and the battle led to dissolution of the Unity Government and *de facto* division of Palestinian territory into two entities – West Bank governed by the PNA and Gaza Strip by Hamas.

Israel launched a military campaign in Gaza Strip in 2008 in response to rocket attacks from Gaza militants, and targeted Palestinian civilians during this campaign. It led to loss of life for at least 115 militants and 150 civilians. United Nations and the European Union condemned Israel for its 'disproportionate use of force'. It was of no consequence to Israel as it had the backing of the United States.

Israel carried out another attack on Gaza Strip in 2014. This time also rocket attack by Hamas militants was shown as the reason for the operation. About 3500 Gazans were killed and 11000 wounded (including 3500 children). About 7000 homes were razed and 10000 damaged. The attack lasted for about two months and ended with a unilateral ceasefire by Israel.

Under United States initiative, Israel normalised relations with four member countries of the Arab League in 2020 – United Arab Emirates, Bahrain, Sudan and Morocco. With this, Israel succeeded in managing recognition and diplomatic relations with six Arab countries, Egypt and Jordan having established diplomatic relations earlier.

The United States prevailed on the Saudi crown prince, and negotiations started at the beginning of 2023 to normalise relations between Saudi Arabia and Israel. In return for normalisation, Saudis wanted a 'defence pact' with the United States, fewer restrictions on US arms sales to Saudi Arabia and assistance in developing its civilian nuclear programme. Creation of a 'Palestinian state' and rehabilitation of Palestinian refugees were other conditions which the Saudis knew would be rejected by Israel but were included to assuage Arab feelings. The negotiations were suspended following the 2023 clash between Israel and the Arabs.

The 2023 clash between Israel and Arabs is the latest in the series of Arab – Israeli conflicts. This time, Israel clashed with Arabs both in the Gaza and West Bank fronts, and the reason advanced is the same – the 'Hamas terrorists'. It is still continuing with both Israel and the United States openly proclaiming that it will continue indefinitely.

Overview

West Asia had been home to ancient civilisations, and Mesopotamia in this region is called the 'cradle of civilisation' by historians. Sumerians, Assyrians, Chaldeans and Phoenicians who made this region the 'cradle' disappeared into the mists of antiquity. They were followed by Jews, Persians, Greeks and Romans. And then came the Arabs to dominate the region.

Jewish culture did not disappear like most others. After they were evicted from their home in the Levant by Romans during the first century AD, they migrated and settled all over the world. They managed to preserve their identity wherever they settled and, after eighteen hundred years, their descendants scattered all over the world got an opportunity to come back, if they desired, to their ancestral home in what is called Palestine today.

Balfour Declaration of 1917 enabled Jews to migrate and settle in Palestine. That was the first step in the fulfilment of Theodor Herzl's dream of a 'homeland' for the Jews. Migration began after Britain established mandatory rule over Palestine, and the Jewish population in Palestine which stood at about forty thousand before 1917 shot up to about five million by 1947.

When mandatory rule ended (1948), Jewish leaders declared the State of Israel and formed their government in the territory they occupied. The United States, The Soviet Union and many European countries recognised it as an independent nation and established diplomatic relations with it. It was admitted as a member state by the United Nations in 1949.

From that time began Jewish territorial expansion and eviction of Arabs from Palestine. About five million Palestinian Arabs had to leave their homes and become refugees in neighbouring countries. They resisted, but resistance was of no use as Israel had the support of western powers, particularly the United States. Having found victory against Israel in regular battle impossible, Arabs switched over to guerilla warfare and terrorist activities. And the Arab-Israeli conflict goes on.

There were other factors too which contributed to the transformation of West Asia into a simmering cauldron.

The region holds almost fifty percent of world's mineral oil deposits. Ever since the discovery of these deposits at the beginning of the twentieth century, western cartels have been active in the region engaging themselves in the exploration and production of petroleum products. Protection of their economic interest was vital for them, and for this, political control of the region was essential. Experience showed that direct political control would be a feeding ground for anti-foreign sentiment, and that led western nations to go by another method – installing pliant regimes of feudal chieftains or ambitious military men which, dependent on western support for survival, would ensure freedom and safety for western ventures. Rank opportunism, interference in internal affairs, political assassinations and interstate wars followed as a direct outcome of this method.

Like other regions, West Asia too was dragged into the Cold War which dominated the latter half of the twentieth century. Following the exit of colonial powers from West Asia after World War II, the United States stepped in to fill the vacuum. The Soviet Union stepped in and tried to checkmate American moves. That brought the two superpowers face to face in West Asia.

Added to this was the rise of Arab nationalism at the beginning of the twentieth century. Most of West Asia was under Ottoman rule for over four hundred years. Slavic people of East European countries were also under Ottoman rule, and, during the nineteenth century, they attained their independence. This inspired the Arabs to think about their independence from Ottoman rule. *Al-Fatat* (Young Arab Society), founded by Arab intellectuals in 1911, marked the commencement of an organised effort for Arab independence. Their claim for establishment of an independent Arab nation was based on their cultural, linguistic and religious identity.

In return for the help against Ottoman Empire during World War I, Britain promised independence for Arabs after the war. Taking this promise in good faith, Arabs cooperated with the British, and their cooperation was of great help in defeating the Ottomans. After the war, however, Britain and France divided West Asian territory vacated by the Ottomans between themselves and began to rule their respective areas under mandates given by the League of Nations. The Arabs felt cheated and became thoroughly anti-west thereafter. This sentiment became a binding factor in their struggle for independence and a stimulant for a pro-Soviet approach in their international relations.

Britain and France earlier, and the United States later, did everything possible to prevent the fulfillment of Arab nationalist aspirations. The colonial powers carved out states in West Asia according to their whims and fancies and encouraged feudal chieftains and ambitious military men to become autocratic rulers in those artificially created states. This was part of a well-designed policy, known as 'divide and rule', which they successfully practised in most colonies to halt or at least slow down the growth of nationalism. These unpopular rulers exploited conservatism and blind religious faith of people for their survival and acted as breakwaters against the rising tide of Arab nationalism, obeying the dictates of their colonial or imperialist masters.

In the name of 'containment of communism', the United States began to interfere in the internal affairs of Arab states. Any ruler who refused to toe the American line ran the risk of being physically eliminated and replaced by a 'pro-American'.

On the face of it, Balfour Declaration represented British sympathy and understanding of the Zionist cause. Jewish claim for Palestine was based on ancestry, that is, Palestine was the ancestral land of the Jews and, therefore, legitimately belonging to them. If ancestry can be the basis for a territorial claim, nothing can prevent Red Indians, Mayas, Incas or Aztecs from claiming America as their land and asking Europeans to vacate, or Maoris claiming New Zealand as their own and asking the British to vacate. Europeans are claiming legitimacy for their occupation of foreign land on the basis of their 'right of conquest'. If Arabs claim Palestine on the same principle, how can they be denied this right?

Balfour Declaration gave promise of help to Jews to migrate and settle in Palestine with the condition that nothing should be done which might prejudice the civil and religious rights of existing non-Jewish communities in Palestine. This condition was, however, 'more honoured in the breach than in the observance', as William Shakespeare said in his play *'Hamlet'*. What actually happened was an enactment of the *'Arab and his camel'* story' – eviction from his tent in which he accommodated his camel. This was being done with the tacit approval of western powers. One day before the British mandate ended, Jewish leaders proclaimed the State of Israel in Palestine, their 'national home' promised in the Balfour Declaration and gained recognition from western nations in no time.

Balfour Declaration was a sham, a sugar-quoted bitter pill, deliberately designed by the British. Their real aim was to have a dagger pointing towards Arab nationalism in West Asia. Jews planted in a hostile environment would be dependent on western patronage for survival and could be used to tackle rising Arab nationalism. That is the only way one can see the British motive in choosing Palestine as the land for Jewish settlement. If their desire was to extend genuine help to the Jews, they could have thought of the United States, Canada, Australia or New Zealand for that purpose as these countries had the capacity to absorb ten times the number of people who migrated and settled in Palestine, without any social disturbance.

A sensible observer may dismiss the Israeli claim that the attack on the Gaza Strip is a retaliatory measure for the 'unprovoked rocket attack by Hamas' as hypocrisy at its extreme. Such excuses are quite familiar. People have heard similar versions on earlier occasions too. American and Israeli leaders have been repeatedly saying that the war will continue indefinitely. Such statements are supplemented by threats from Israeli extremists that it would be better if Arabs vacated Gaza Strip and West Bank. The intention is quite clear. Israeli adventure will continue till the conquest of Gaza Strip and West Bank is completed and the last Arab driven out of Palestine.

For the Palestinian Arabs, it is time to realise that 'peace plans' brokered by anyone, including the United Nations, are meaningless. They have two options: either accept injustice and insult heaped on them meekly and live as refugees in neighbouring countries, or continue their struggle and live or die with honour and dignity.

If the Arabs think that their present leadership will take them to their desired goal, they are living in an illusory world. They need a leader like Ho Chi Minh or Fidel Castro to lead them.

Palestine has become the most difficult problem for West Asia. Until this problem and other problems left by colonialism and economic imperialism are solved satisfactorily, there can be no lasting peace in this region.

Map of Palestine

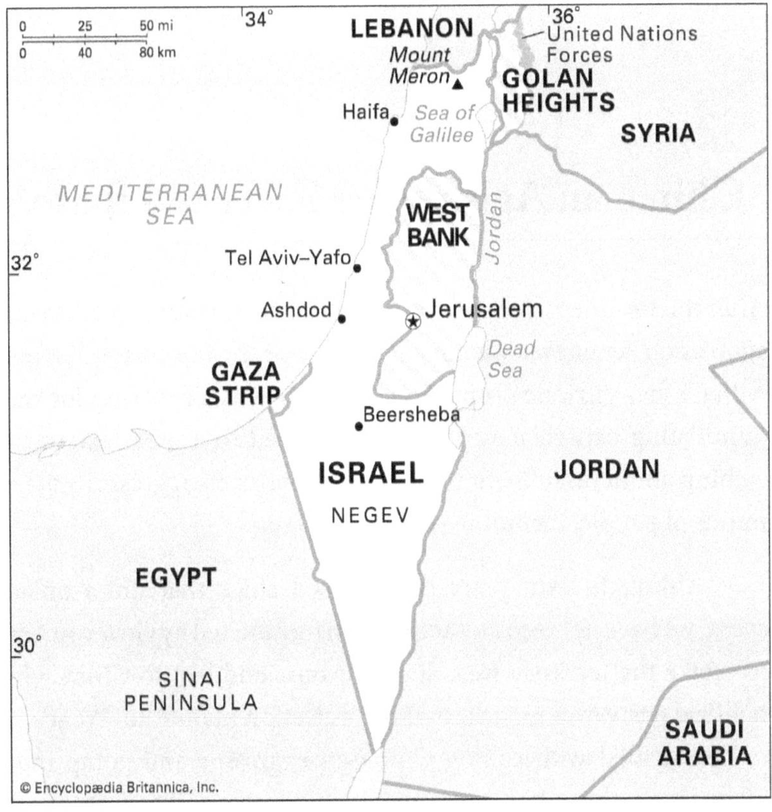

China, an Aggressor? Facts and fiction

After the 1962 debacle, it became a fashion to use the term 'Chinese aggression' whenever we talked of Tibet or the boundary dispute with China. Vitriolic propaganda unleashed as a cover-up for the humiliating experiences of 1962 succeeded to a great extent in etching an inerasable impression of China as an aggressor in the minds of people, including the educated ones.

Although sixty years have passed since that unfortunate event, we have not seen any action plan formulated by Government to retake the territory we claimed as ours and lost to China. No political party ever made it part of its election manifesto. We seem to be satisfied with calling China an aggressor and going into hibernation thereafter. Occasionally, we see a military standoff on the borders followed by farcical conferences of military commanders to 'ease tension'. They end up with charges and countercharges over an imaginary line called 'the line of actual control (LAC)'. We allow the Dalai Lama to make occasional appearances reminding of 'Chinese aggression' over Tibet. What purpose it serves, no one knows.

It is high time that educated people take a second look at the whole issue instead of being misled by propaganda meant to cover up past mistakes. Introspection and self-criticism would be helpful in rectification of omissions, if any, on our part.

China and Tibet

Ensconced in the Himalayas, Tibet had very little contact with outside world in ancient times. Tibetan people claim Mongoloid origin, and, to begin with, were animistic in their beliefs and practices. *Mahayana* Buddhism reached Tibet in the second century AD through Kashgar and Khotan (Xinjiang region of China) and began exercising a powerful influence on the life and culture of Tibetan people. Buddhist scholars travelling from Tibet to India and *vice versa* which started after Buddhism became well-established in Tibet must have naturally led to cultural exchanges between the two countries since then.

The warring tribes of Mongolia got unified under Genghis Khan, and they began their territorial expansion in the thirteenth century. Mongol forays into the Tibetan region started from this time. Tibet had no central Government in those days, and raids were directed against local chieftains and wealthy monasteries, the aim being plundering and looting almost always. Intensity of raids increased with the passage of time, and by the time Kublai Khan, grandson of Genghis Khan, became the Mongol Emperor (1260), most Tibetan chieftains were subdued and made to accept Mongol overlordship.

Mongols invaded China in the thirteenth century, and, crushing all opposing regional powers, established their sway over major part of China by the middle of the century. Kublai Khan crowned himself as the Emperor of China and established Yuan dynastic rule over China which lasted from 1271 to 1368. The Khan made Tibet part of his Chinese Empire and established a patron-priest relationship with the Lamas of Tibet. That meant military and administrative control in the Khan's hands and a measure of autonomy in spiritual matters for Tibetans.

By the middle of the fourteenth century, Yuan Empire began to disintegrate, and control over outlying regions like Tibet began to weaken. Ming Dynasty succeeded Yuan Dynasty, and Ming rule lasted from 1368 to 1644.

Modern Chinese historians assert that China had unquestioned sovereignty over Tibet during the Ming period and point out the issue of titles by Ming Emperors to Tibetan chieftains and officials, acceptance of such titles by recipients and the renewal process of titles which involved title holders travelling to Ming capital as evidence in support of their contention. However, western historians dispute this claim on the ground that supporting evidence is inadequate and unreliable. Whatever be the merits and demerits of these claims, one thing is certain. No power seems to have come forward in Tibet during the Ming period challenging Chinese sovereignty over Tibet. We may, therefore, assume that arrangements made during the Yuan period continued without any perceptible change during the Ming period.

A noticeable development in Tibetan religious life during this period was the emergence of the Gelugpa School of Buddhism as the leading religious denomination. Sonam Gyatso (1543-1588), a monk of the Gelugpa tradition and Abbot of Drepung Monastery near Lhasa (capital of Tibet), became a popular religious leader with the help and patronage of Altan Khan (1507-1582), the Tumed Mongol Chief and a descendant of Genghis Khan. The Khan bestowed the title 'Dalai Lama'

(Dalai means ocean and Lama means teacher) on Sonam who claimed himself to be Avalokiteswara, a *Brahmmana* associate of Gautama Buddha, in his rebirth. His successors (selected on 'revelation' basis) followed the tradition of being known as Dalai Lama. Zhu Yijun, the fourteenth Ming Emperor, honoured Sonam with the title 'Dorji Chang' (*Vajradhara*) in 1587 and gave him the seal of authority.

Sonam was considered third in the line of Dalai Lamas, the first and second places have been posthumously conferred on his predecessors (Gendun Drup and Gendun Gyatso respectively) found out on revelation basis. He was succeeded by Altan Khan's great-grandson Yonten Gyatso (1589-1617) as the fourth Dalai Lama, and Yonten Gyatso was succeeded by Lobsang Gyatso (1617-1682) as the fifth in the line.

Following the death of the fourth Dalai Lama, conflict broke out between different religious groups in Tibet. Lobsang found a patron in Gushi Khan, the Koshut Mongol Chief and a descendant of Qasar, younger brother of Genghis Khan. Gushi Khan intervened and succeeded in bringing the Civil War to an end. He also restored the supremacy of the Gelugpa School. This led to the Dalai Lama being accepted as the undisputed spiritual leader of all Tibetans from the time of the fifth Dalai Lama.

Qing (Manchu) Dynasty succeeded Ming Dynasty, and effective Qing rule over China began in 1644. In 1653, the Dalai Lama visited the Qing court at Peking (modern Beijing) and was honoured by the Emperor as the spiritual authority of the Qing Empire. The Emperor presumably acted under the belief that China-Tibet relations established during Yuan rule had remained unchanged.

Nothing happened during the next twenty years to change that belief. But the non-cooperative attitude of the Dalai Lama in crushing the revolt of vassals in the Yunnan region of China during the 1670s angered the Emperor, and when the Mongols of Dzungar Khanate invaded Tibet in 1717, he did not seek the Dalai Lama's assistance. Instead, he sent his own force and drove the invaders out. To prevent further invasions, political control was taken over and an army contingent stationed in Lhasa. A representative of the Imperial Government (Amban) was kept in Lhasa to oversee political administration of Tibet. In spiritual matters, autonomy allowed during Yuan rule continued. Tibet was thus brought once again under the effective control of the Chinese Imperial Government by the Qing Emperor during the eighteenth century.

The Opium Wars and extra-territorial concessions imposed on China by foreign powers during the nineteenth century led to the weakening and ultimate disintegration of the Qing Empire. Control over outlying regions of the Empire, including Tibet, became ineffective as a result of this overall decay. However, the vassal-suzerain relationship between these regions and China seems to have remained unaffected till the beginning of the twentieth century. In the treaty of 1906 signed between Britain and China and in the Anglo-Russian Convention of 1907, Chinese suzerainty over Tibet was recognised by Britain and Russia. Both powers agreed that they would not interfere in the internal affairs of Tibet, and, without the knowledge and approval of China, no negotiations would be conducted with Tibet.

Taking advantage of the weakness of China, the Dalai Lama tried to assert independence and approached foreign powers for help. He failed in this attempt as no help came from anywhere.

He had to give up his pretensions when the Imperial Government moved troops to reassert sovereignty over Tibet following the British attempt to enter Lhasa and dictate terms to the Tibetan administration in 1904.

Following Emperor Puyi's abdication in 1912, Manchu dynastic rule came to an end in China, and the Nationalist Party of China headed by Dr Sun Yat-sen assumed power. The Dalai Lama once again came up with his claim for Tibetan independence. Declaring himself as the spiritual and temporal ruler of Tibet in 1913, he expelled the imperial representative (Amban) from Tibet and ordered Chinese people living in Lhasa to leave Tibet within the time allowed by him. Although the Nationalist Government claimed the title to rule the entire Qing territory including Tibet as the legal successor to the Qing Government, it was too weak to exercise real authority over the territory claimed, and the Dalai Lama continued with his title and claim till the communist takeover of 1949.

The primary task of the Communist regime after assumption of power was territorial consolidation. There were still pockets of Nationalist resistance to be cleared by use of force where necessary. Outlying regions had been virtually independent for nearly half a century due to inability of the central administration to exercise effective control over them. Chinese leadership had to face the dissidents squarely to ensure the successful implementation of this policy. Of all the problems China had to face, the Tibetan issue was the toughest.

China wanted integration of Tibet with the rest of China in a peaceful manner. But the Dalai Lama's refusal to come to terms hardened its attitude. In October 1950, Chinese army crossed the Jinsha River and captured the border town of Chamdo (eastern Tibet). Instead of continuing with the military operation, China asked Tibet to send representatives to Beijing to negotiate a settlement. Agreeing to this proposal, the Tibetan local government sent representatives, and negotiations between the two sides led to the signing of an agreement in 1951.

According to the terms of this agreement, Tibet would become an integral part of China with the right to exercise regional autonomy under the unified leadership of the Central Government. Religious beliefs and traditions would be respected, and monasteries protected. Tibetan troops would be integrated with the People's Liberation Army and would become part of the People's Republic of China's defence forces. The Dalai Lama ratified this agreement by a telegram in October 1951.

The Dalai Lama had no intention to abide by this agreement even though he ratified it, and started seeking foreign assistance to free Tibet from Chinese control. This gave the United States, engaged in destabilising communist regimes all over the world, an opportunity to intervene. In India, there were people who perceived the communist advance into Tibet as a threat to their vested interests, and they were 'sympathetic' to the Dalai Lama. The United States felt that direct involvement would pose problems and planned to route assistance through India. However, India did not want to be seen as openly acting against Chinese interests. Assistance, therefore, took a clandestine form and was confined to training and equipping rebels for guerilla warfare secretly outside Tibet.

For China, the Dalai Lama's ratification of the agreement signalled undisputed integration of Tibet with China. On that understanding, China began land reforms in Tibet as part of its overall socialist reconstruction programme. That involved taking over surplus land from landholders and redistributing it among landless peasants. The dispossessed landholders (Lamas of monasteries and aristocrats) rose in revolt against this move, and the rebellion which started in the eastern provinces of Kham and Amdo in 1956 spread to the rest of Tibet soon. With active assistance from outside powers, the rebellion reached alarming proportions by 1959 forcing China to intervene militarily. Fearing for his life, the Dalai Lama fled the country and took asylum in India. On his way to India, he repudiated the agreement signed by him in 1951 saying that it was forced on Tibet.

The anti-communist lobby backed by corporate-controlled media lost no time in picking up the episode, blowing it up and using it to portray China as an 'aggressor' and the Dalai Lama as the 'victim' of 'Chinese aggression'.

Prime Minister Nehru made a statement in Indian Parliament clarifying the position in reply to questions from opposition members. He reminded them that Tibet had been part of China since the thirteenth century, and what happened in the 1950s was only a reassertion of authority which was lost during its weak stage. Defence Minister Krishna Menon went a step further and said that reassertion of authority on own territory did not amount to aggression in terms of the United Nations Charter.

India too had to face similar problems when it began its journey as an independent nation. An important problem was the integration of princely states with the Indian Union. The Transfer of Power Agreement of 1947 gave freedom to princely states to choose either India or Pakistan for accession. While majority of the states decided to accede to India or Pakistan, taking into consideration geographical contiguity, Junagadh acceded to Pakistan, ignoring the geographical factor, and Hyderabad decided to remain independent (an option not provided in the Agreement). In both cases, India had to use force for their accession to India. *Nawab* of Junagadh and *Vazir* of Hyderabad fled their states and sought asylum in Pakistan. No one came forward at that time to call India an aggressor or those who escaped to Pakistan victims of Indian aggression.

Next was Goa. Goa, a part of the Bijapur Sultanate, came under Portuguese control during the early part of the sixteenth century. India was only a geographical concept then (It became a political entity only after the British brought conquered territories south of the Himalayas under a single administrative set-up during the middle of the nineteenth century). French and Portuguese possessions in the subcontinent continued along with British-controlled territory by virtue of agreements between the mother countries. As the legal successor to the colonial Government, India could claim only the territory transferred to it under the Transfer of Power Agreement of 1947. French and Portuguese possessions were not part of the transferred territory, and India could not advance any legal claim on them. The French willingly gave their possessions to India, but the Portuguese did not. That led to the military action (codenamed 'Operation Vijay') of 1961 and takeover of Goa. No one came forward to call India an aggressor this time too.

Caught in the post-1962 propaganda blitz, the average Indian lost sight of such arguments. The fact that the Dalai Lama was recognised only as a spiritual leader and the temporal power he assumed was illegal was also pushed under the mat. Ignoring all these facts, people were made to believe that China invaded Tibet and thereby became an 'aggressor'.

Boundary Dispute

Unfortunately, important classified documents relating to the boundary dispute remain to be declassified and thrown open to the public. We have, therefore, to grope in the dark in certain areas, and our observations relating to those areas tend to be speculative. That is a point to be borne in mind when we discuss this issue.

Sino-Indian border, about 3500 kilometres long, was never properly demarcated on the ground. Of this, the only section on which both countries agree that there is no dispute is the 220 kilometre long Sikkim-Tibet boundary agreed upon in the Anglo-Chinese Convention of 1890.

In the western sector, territorial claims of India and China overlapped. India claimed Ladakh including Aksai Chin as its territory. China disputed this and asserted that Aksai Chin was part of Tibet and, therefore, Chinese territory. These claims were based on traditions and old maps.

In the Treaty of Chushul (1842) signed by representatives of Qing China and the ruler of Jammu and Kashmir, both sides agreed to 'respect the ancient boundary between Ladakh and Tibet'. The 'ancient boundary' referred to was apparently the boundary mentioned in the Treaty of Tingmosgang (1684) which ran along the Lhari stream and Demchok. It is not clear whether Aksai Chin was part of Ladakh at that time. Tradition and old maps could provide support only to this extent.

The question of demarcating the border in the western sector came up for active consideration of the colonial Government when a Russian invasion of India through Xinjiang and Tibet appeared a possibility in British political thinking. After an elaborate survey, two lines were suggested as the boundary between Jammu-Kashmir and Tibet. One line (Ardag line of 1897) passed through the Kunlun Range while the other line (Macartney-Macdonald line of 1899) followed the Karakorum alignment. The latter excluded Aksai Chin from the Indian side. Eventually, a note was sent to China in 1899 defining the limits of India for the purpose of a boundary with China on the basis of the Macartney-Macdonald line. China did not respond to this, and that was taken as an excuse for revising the line later to suit colonial interests. With the collapse of Tsarist Russia during the early part of the twentieth century, the fear of Russian invasion vanished, and the border issue in the western sector lost heat.

In the eastern sector also claims overlapped. China's claim was that the southern boundary of Tibet in the eastern sector followed the base of the foothills of the Himalayas, and, therefore, the region which is now known as Arunachal Pradesh lying north of this line would be part of Tibet. India disputed this claim and claimed McMahon line as the boundary between India and Tibet. Since this line followed the crests of the foothills, Arunachal Pradesh, lying south of this line, would be Indian Territory. While China relied on tradition as backup for its claim, India took the agreement of 1914 between Tibet and the colonial Government as its support base.

It is necessary to go a little more into details at this stage to have a clear idea of McMahon line and its relevance. After the First Anglo-Burmese War (1824-1826), Brahmaputra valley of Assam came under East India company's control. Over the next few decades, the area was extended without any clear demarcation of boundary between the extended territory and Tibet lying north. China became suspicious of British intentions and responded with its own forward policy which involved taking control of the south-eastern region of Tibet through which passed China's line of communication with Tibet. This move alarmed British political circles, and, by 1912, they came to the conclusion that it was time the boundary between colonial India and Tibet was demarcated in the eastern sector.

Under British initiative, a conference was arranged at Simla (now Shimla) in 1913 to demarcate the boundary. Representatives of Britain, China and Tibet participated in the conference. During the discussion, the British delegation presented a map showing the proposed boundary line which took the name 'McMahon line' after Sir Henry McMahon, Foreign Secretary of colonial India at that time and chief negotiator at the conference. The line began from the northeastern border of Bhutan and, following the crests of the Himalayas, ended with the north-western border of Burma (about 890 kilometres long) making Arunachal Pradesh part of colonial India.

Chinese delegation refused to accept this boundary on the ground that Tibetan territory extended up to the base of the foothills of the Himalayas. As Tibetan delegation accepted it, British delegation signed the agreement with Tibet, and that agreement came to be known as the Simla Agreement of 1914. China refused to recognise this agreement on the ground that Tibet, being a vassal state of China, had no authority to sign an agreement with anyone without the approval of China, and China had not given approval.

Too weak to enforce its claim, China could do nothing more than express dissent at that time. British delegation ignored this dissent. By virtue of this agreement, McMahon line became the *de facto* boundary between colonial India and Tibet, and Arunachal Pradesh claimed by China as its territory became Indian Territory.

India attained independence in 1947 and moved on to establish a liberal democratic republic on western model. Two years later, communists assumed power in China replacing nationalists and adopted the Marxist model for shaping China's future. In spite of ideological differences, the age-old cordial relation between the two countries continued. The unsettled border and overlapping territorial claims did not figure as serious issues at that time.

But this honeymoon did not last long. Chinese advance into Tibet following ratification of the 1951 agreement by the Dalai Lama was, for the powerful anti-communist lobby in India, a communist advance up to India's doorstep and, therefore, not welcome. The influence of this lobby began to weigh heavily on India's relationship with China thereafter. Even though mutual respect for each other's territorial integrity, non-interference in internal affairs, nonaggression and peaceful coexistence were highlighted in the *Panchsheel* Agreement signed by India and China in 1954, these principles remained on paper, and matters went from bad to worse in the years that followed.

China's use of force to quell the revolt in Tibet and the Dalai Lama's taking asylum in India aggravated the situation, and the deteriorating relation reached a point of no return by 1960. At that stage the Chinese Prime Minister Zhou en-Lai came to India and made what could be considered as the last effort to settle the border dispute through negotiation with his Indian counterpart. During their meeting in April 1960, China presented a 'package deal' for the solution of the border dispute in a give-and-take manner.

According to this deal, China would keep Aksai Chin claimed by it and, in return, forego its claim on the territory south of the McMahon line in the northeast. It was ready to take Aksai Chin even on a lease basis if it was embarrassing for India to agree to a permanent transfer. India refused to accept this proposal and asserted that its claim on Aksai Chin and Arunachal Pradesh could not be compromised. Chinese Prime Minister returned empty-handed, and that signalled a hardening of Chinese attitude towards India. Thereafter, China was not ready for any compromise on its earlier claim on both Aksai Chin and Arunachal Pradesh.

What prompted China to come up with this package deal which involved foregoing claim on Arunachal Pradesh for the sake of a comparatively smaller piece of land, Aksai Chin? It was even ready to take it on lease basis even though there was no record establishing India's ownership beyond doubt. In the absence of reliable records, whatever answer we find out can only be speculative.

On the face of it, it indicated an emergency necessitating a settlement at any cost. What could be that emergency?

On the eastern side of Tibet, the line of communication between China and Tibet passed through rugged mountain ranges, and journey through this route was hazardous and time - consuming. On the northern side, there was no connectivity at all. The western side provided better conditions. A caravan route connecting Tibet and Xinjiang region of China existed on this side from early times, and it passed through the Aksai Chin region. China was using this route without any hindrance.

To facilitate fast movement of men and materials, China decided to construct a road to replace the old caravan route. Construction of this road which seems to have begun sometime in 1951 took almost seven years to complete. It remained the only dependable line of communication between China and Tibet till China developed alternate arrangements later. When a formal announcement was made by China after the completion of the road, India sent an informal note to China complaining that China had not sought India's permission to construct the road in the region claimed as India's territory. China's reaction was that this had been the traditional route connecting Xinjiang and Tibet, and the road followed the same route. The fact that India never protested in the past was eloquent proof for China to assume that this region was within its jurisdiction.

If China were to accept India's claim it would have lost control over that portion of the road which passed through the Aksai Chin region (about 120 kilometres long) which it could not afford in the context of the Tibetan revolt backed by outside powers. Control over this vital line of communication could, therefore, be a possible reason behind the idea of a settlement at any cost.

Some political observers have come forward lately with the opinion that India missed a golden opportunity for settlement of the border dispute with China when it rejected the Chinese offer. True, India would have lost a few square kilometres of territory in the Aksai Chin region claimed as Indian Territory. But it would have gained, in return, recognition of McMahon line as the *de jure* boundary in the eastern sector between India and Tibetan part of China, undisputed possession of areas south of this line

(Arunachal Pradesh) and a peaceful border all along. The sacrifice was too small for such a big gain.

Succumbing to pressure exerted by vested interests, political leadership in India took an unreasonable attitude. The United States and Canada, Soviet Union and Iran and People's Republic of China and Burma had boundary disputes like this, but they were all solved amicably through negotiation on a give-and-take basis. India also could have solved this problem in a similar manner. If future historians pass an unfavourable verdict on the Indian political leadership which handled this issue, they cannot be faulted.

Chinese Prime Minister's return marked the end of peaceful coexistence, and heralded the era of hostility between India and China. The unmarked boundary between the two countries for the most part passed through uninhabited barren land in the Himalayas where the temperature dipped to −30 degrees Celsius in winter, particularly in the western sector. This made control and supervision of areas through which the assumed boundary passed difficult. Yet by 1956, both sides started sending patrols to supervise 'boundary violations' in the areas claimed as own territory. Where the claims overlapped, patrolling became 'encroachments' and when tension began to increase, such encroachments led to armed conflicts and finally to war.

After militarily taking over areas claimed as own territory in 1962, China declared a unilateral ceasefire and returned Indian soldiers taken prisoner during the war. It was a humiliating experience for India. No serious effort was made to settle the dispute thereafter. Borders in the eastern and western sectors have remained volatile ever since with the possibility of open hostility erupting any time. Both sides swear by a 'line of actual control (LAC)' which in fact is a fiction because there is no such line on any map and it varies according to each side's perception.

Historians may record this only as a boundary dispute, not aggression, since both sides claimed only what was considered as own territory. Aggression, as normally understood, involves forcible occupation of territory belonging to another country without any legal or moral claim on it.

Overview

From what is stated above, it will be clear that the word 'aggression' does not fit in with Chinese action in Tibet or the boundary dispute between India and China. In the case of Tibet, it was only a reassertion of authority on own territory; in the case of the boundary dispute, it was only an unfortunate clash arising from overlapping territorial claims. And yet, most people including the educated ones use that term as a matter of course. Consistent indoctrination by the establishment led to making it an obsession for some. Those who hold different opinions are afraid of expressing them, as they think that they would be branded anti-national if they express their honest opinion. It is only in some unprejudiced intellectual circles that we can look for a bold assertion of truth.

India and China had cordial relations in the past. Buddhism which reached China in the second century AD helped to build a cultural bridge between the two ancient civilisations. Buddhist scholars like Fa-hien from China visited India, and Indian scholars reciprocated with their visit to China. These visits led not only to exchange of ideas but also to strengthening the bond of friendship based on mutual respect and admiration.

Side by side was trade relation between the two countries which began during the Han period (206 BC to 220 AD). As observed by travellers like Marco Polo and Ibn Batuta, a number of trade centres flourished on the Kerala coast of India to handle the large transoceanic trade between the two countries. This trade relationship lasted till the beginning of the colonial era.

under colonial rule, both countries went through more or less similar experiences. While the British made India their colony, several western powers carved out 'spheres of influence' in China. Imperial Japan was an additional menace for China. Both countries suffered heavily during the colonial era, and that suffering brought them closer to each other.

A few instances illustrating this cordial relationship can be mentioned here. During the Japanese invasion of China in 1938, India sent a medical mission to China as a token of friendship. One of the doctors in the team died while serving in China. He was held in high esteem in China, and it was a practice for Chinese leaders visiting India to visit his family and pay their respects personally. When Indian Vice President late Dr Radhakrishnan was flying to Japan on a goodwill visit over the China Sea in the 1950s, Chinese guns pounding Taiwan stopped firing and dipped in salute as a mark of respect. When the *Panchsheel* agreement was signed by India and China in 1954, people rejoiced, and '*Hindi Cheeni bhai bhai*' became a pet slogan in the Indian mind. When the Chinese Prime Minister visited India in 1956 and came to Bombay (now Mumbai), a million-strong crowd thronged to see him. India was one of the earliest countries to recognise People's Republic of China and sponsor China's membership in the United Nations.

This friendly relationship snapped overnight as a result of the malicious propaganda campaign. 'Chinese aggression' and Chinese 'betrayal' began to get embedded in the minds of gullible Indians thereafter. For the Chinese people, a feeling that 'India can never be trusted' was the reaction.

We still linger on in the make-believe world we created after 1962. It is time we have a rethink on the whole issue. An important factor we have to bear in mind is that enmity with China is not in the best interest of our country. It creates a feeling of insecurity, and that leads to ever-increasing defence expenditure and consequent strain on our scarce resources. Along with it arises the necessity of aligning with other powerful countries to counter the imagined threat from China which takes away our freedom to pursue independent policies in the international arena. In no way less important is the trade relation between the two countries. As per published statistics, the value of India's imports from China for the year 2023-24 amounted to over 101 billion US dollars. A flare-up and consequent disruption in trade can paralyse our electronic, pharmaceutical, chemical and automobile industries and cripple our economy.

The sooner we settle the border dispute with China amicably, the better for us.

Democracy as a Political Institution

To a question what he understood by the term 'democracy', a young man's answer was 'government of the people by the people for the people'. He was not sure who said it. He had apparently taken it as the universally accepted definition of democracy. Most political and social organisations have the word 'democratic' tagged on to their names, presumably under the belief that such tagging would enhance their prestige and earn greater acceptance among people. Some people think that political institutions of countries like the United States, England or India are 'democratic' while those that do not fit in exactly with this pattern are 'dictatorships', another term as vaguely understood as democracy.

The words 'of the people, by the people, for the people' were part of the speech delivered by President Abraham Lincoln of the United States during the dedication of the Soldiers' National Cemetery in Gettysburg, Pennsylvania (US) in 1863, and were used in relation to the government formed by the settlers in 1775. The word democracy does not find a place in it.

Multi-party system with a titular head of state is the distinguishing feature of the political institutions of the United States, England or India. Liberalism in economic activity is another distinguishing feature. For votaries of this system, all other forms of government are 'undemocratic'. These 'undemocratic' governments are styled 'dictatorship', 'totalitarian', 'autocratic' etc, no matter what justification followers of those systems have for their choice.

To understand the scope and content of democracy, it would be necessary to trace its course from the beginning.

Origin and Development of Democracy

The term 'democracy' has a Greek origin, 'demo' meaning people and 'cracy' meaning governance. Translated into English, it would mean 'people's government'. Democracy as a political institution began in its rudimentary form in Greece in the sixth century BC.

Greek Civilisation which emerged after the Dark Age (1000 BC to 700 BC) began in small settlements of people (city-states or *polis*) under chieftains. During the sixth century BC, a 'tyrant' called Peisistratus 'usurped' power in the city-state of Athens and tried to impose his 'despotic' rule over people. With the help of the city-state of Sparta, the Athenians drove him out. Trouble for Athens, however, did not end there. Sparta used this opportunity to install a 'puppet' regime in Athens with the intention of bringing Athens under Sparta's control. Athenians found their survival as an independent state threatened by this move. At this juncture, the Athenian aristocrat Cleisthenes called upon Athenian citizens to come forward, keeping aside their rank and status, and form a government of their own to face the situation. They responded positively and formed a government which succeeded in defeating the Spartans and putting an end to their design. The government formed by the Athenian citizens was on 'democratic' principles.

Only adult male members of Athenian landowning families were 'citizens' for this democracy. Rest of Athenian society (including women) constituting about two-thirds of the population were denied participation. The citizens assembled at a chosen place and took decisions on state matters on the basis of majority (in the absence of unanimity). Implementation of decisions was the responsibility of men chosen by the citizens from among themselves.

In contrast to the monarchical institutions obtaining in contemporary societies, the institution of democracy which took shape in Athens recognised law as the basis of governance and brought out a well-defined legal system as its support base. Draco and Solon of Athens stand out as the earliest lawgivers of ancient Greece. Courts were established for trial, conviction and award of punishment. People familiar with law could be engaged for prosecution and defence. Offices like *archon* (magistrate) and *polymath* (general) came into existence for administration of justice.

It is interesting to note here that for philosophers like Plato who lived during this period, the 'democratic experiment' of Athens was not in line with their way of thinking. It was, according to them, nothing more than a show by hypocrites who managed affairs with their empty 'rhetoric', and it would lead to nothing but 'tyranny'.

The democratic experiment of Athens attracted attention of people, and other city-states emulated this experiment. The Peloponnesian Wars that raged during the Classic Period (500 BC to 323 BC) put severe stress on the institution of democracy. Somehow, it survived overcoming attempts to replace it with other forms of government. With the Roman conquest of Greece in the first century BC, the city-states lost their independence and became local bodies within the Roman Empire. With this, the democratic experiment ended in Greece.

Roman civilisation which began in the eighth century BC with Romulus as the chieftain continued with its monarchical form of government till the sixth century BC, and then switched over to an aristocratic republic. Government formed by the republic was on democratic principles similar to those of the Greek city-states.

The realisation that concentration of power in the hands of an individual or a group of persons would lead to arbitrariness made the Romans think in terms of widening the scope of democracy to cover different groups in society. Three different organs, namely, the term-limited elected *consul*, the *senate* and the *comitia*, representing the monarchical, aristocratic and popular elements respectively, were created as parts of government. Each organ had its specified functions. That was an innovation on the principles followed by the Greeks who thought of the institution as that of the aristocrats alone.

As in the case of the Greek city-states, adult male citizens alone had participation in Roman democracy. The *senate* was dominated by *patricians* (those who could trace their ancestry to one of the hundred *patriarchs* who founded Rome) and they held real power. The *consul* would be elected from among the *senators*. The *comitia* (assembly) was meant for *plebeians* (other adult male freeborn citizens) and had only a limited role. Women and slaves constituting about thirty percent of the population had no participation.

A well-defined legal system became the support base for Roman democracy also. Roman legal system was perhaps the earliest to recognise natural justice and common sense as the basis of law. Laws protecting interest of the state (public law) as distinguished from laws protecting citizens' rights (private law), review of decisions of lower authority by higher authority, laws relating to ownership and possession, laws relating to contractual obligations, legality of will and testament etc were novel features of the Roman legal system.

The democratic experiment in Rome lasted for about five hundred years. In the first century BC, Octavian, grandnephew and adopted son of Julius Caesar, replaced democracy with absolute monarchy, and attempts to revive it thereafter did not succeed.

As revealed by Buddhist literature, in ancient India too, a democratic experiment similar to that of the Greco-Roman model was attempted beginning from about the sixth century BC. While most Aryan settlements went in for the monarchical form of government, few settlements like those of the Lichavies, Mallas and the Kolyas tried the republican form of polity. Instead of the hereditary monarch, an elected leader became the head of state in these republics. We do not have information about the method of election or the tenure of the elected leader. In the same way, we are in the dark about the functioning of the government in these republics.

One thing is, however, certain. Caste system having been well established in Aryan society by this time, administration and defence would have been in the hands of the Kshatriya caste, and the leader could have been elected only from this caste. That would have made the government look like an oligarchy. The *panchayat* system, with each caste having its own set up with elders deciding issues of that caste on the basis of traditions, customs and practices, independent of the central government, which had developed by this time would have gone along with the republican form at the top which presumably decided matters pertaining to the settlement as a whole.

By about the first century BC, the republics disappeared giving way to the monarchical form of government. Along with them disappeared the democratic experiment also.

With the decline and fall of the Greco-Roman civilisation, the idea of democracy disappeared from Europe. It was rediscovered by European thinkers while going through Greek and Roman literature during the Renaissance Age, and the period that followed witnessed the idea being put on trial once again.

Democracy of Modern Times

The trial began in England first. Post-Norman conquest monarchs of England had an advisory council of bishops and barons, known as *Magnum Concilium* (The Great Council), to advise them while taking important decisions. From about the fifteenth century, kings began to instruct sheriffs of counties to depute knights of shires and boroughs to take part in the proceedings of the Council. This Council came to be known as 'Parliament' later with a 'House of Lords' for bishops and barons and a 'House of Commons' for the knights who were known as 'commoners'.

Tudor monarchs who ruled England during the sixteenth century were autocrats. They often bypassed the Council and summoned it only when they wanted to get through with unpopular measures like fresh taxation. The commoners would be the worst hit by such measures, particularly when it came to the imposition of taxes. The entire burden would fall on them, as bishops and barons enjoyed protection under their immunities and privileges. Naturally, such measures faced resistance from the commoners.

Confrontation between the monarch and the House of Commons reached its climax during the Stuart era (seventeenth century) and led to an open fight between the two during the middle of the century. With the victory of the commoners in the Civil War, absolute monarchy came to an end, and, guided by the ideas of Renaissance Age thinkers, England settled for a 'constitutional monarchy' and 'democratic' form of government.

Under the new arrangement, the monarch became a titular head of state. Bishops and barons with curtailed immunities and privileges continued in the House of Lords by virtue of their ecclesiastical position or appointment as peers. Elected representatives of people sat as members of the House of Commons. Election was through secret ballot, and only taxpayers would be eligible to vote. The representative system was an innovation on the Greco-Roman model. As a result of this change, political power and control over state finance, prerogatives of the nobility and the clergy during the Middle Ages, passed on to the middle-order of society consisting of traders and small-scale landholders who constituted the taxpaying members of English society. Large number of people (including women), the non-taxpayers, remained outside the system.

The experiment that began in England became a model for other countries. The thirteen British colonies of North America which broke away from Britain after the War of Independence formed a 'democratic' republic in 1775. France moved on to form its government on 'democratic' principles after dismantling the monarchical state during the French Revolution.

These 'democratic' ideas were, in fact, an intellectual reaction against monarchical absolutism and autocratic rule, a characteristic feature of the feudal age. They assumed a moral high ground by identifying with the ideas of philosophers like

John Locke, Jean-Jacques Rousseau and Tom Paine who spoke of the 'inalienable rights of man' and 'equality before the law' and believed that a government formed by people alone could protect these rights and ensure equality.

Industrial Revolution of the eighteenth-nineteenth century changed earlier social equations. Two new groups emerged in society, one formed by industrial entrepreneurs and the other by wage-earning labourers. Through their elected representatives in the House of Commons, they too became contestants for political power. Formation of parties with definite political and socio-economic programmes, election of members on party basis and formation of government by party commanding majority in the House of Commons followed as innovatory steps.

The democratic system which began in England in the seventeenth century and spread to other countries during the succeeding centuries enabled the middle-order people (traders and small-scale landholders) to assert their inalienable rights and claim equality before the law to a great extent. Constitutions backing up their systems, written or unwritten, guaranteed these rights, and the executive ensured their implementation.

As human society moved on to the twentieth century, political observers began to see contradictions and shortcomings in the democratic system practised in Europe and America. European settlers in America clamouring for democratic rights and privileges for themselves were denying basic rights as human beings to enslaved people of African origin. European countries going ahead with their democratic experiment at home never thought of discontinuing autocratic rule in their colonies in Asia and Africa. Tax restrictions for the elections made large number of people including women ineligible for participation in the system.

Collective wisdom of human beings corrected these aberrations as twentieth century advanced. People of African origin freed from slavery in the United States started gaining recognition as human beings and a semblance of democratic rights. Other slave-owning societies also followed this example. Countries freed from colonial rule were able to form governments of their choice, and many of them formed their governments on 'democratic' basis. Tax restriction was removed, and universal adult franchise became the basis for election.

Philosophers of the seventeenth and eighteenth centuries were of the opinion that overall development of the individual was a must for social progress, and for this development, removal of constraints on individual freedom was a prerequisite. This idea became the cornerstone of the democratic experiment in Europe and America. The end of monarchical absolutism and feudal privileges paved the way for the removal of obstacles in the way of this freedom. Specific provisions for individual freedom find their place in the constitutions or legal systems of countries which adopted the democratic form of government. This freedom included, among other things, freedom of expression and belief and the right to own property.

As the democratic experiment progressed, the concept of individual freedom came under critical examination of thinkers. While it was considered essential for self-development, they felt that it could not be unlimited. If individual freedom clashed with social freedom, the former had to be subordinated to the latter as otherwise social existence would be impossible. At the primitive stage of human beings, one could imagine something very near the concept of absolute individual freedom. Social progress necessitated progressive curtailment of that freedom. To the extent it was lost, it came back in the form of social freedom.

Equality of human beings was another issue stressed by philosophers of the seventeenth and eighteenth centuries. To meet this demand, legal systems of countries which adopted the democratic form of government made provisions for equality before law. That led to the introduction of universal adult franchise or 'one person, one vote' principle in the election of representatives. It did not take much time for those who critically examined the issue to realise that equality before law could make people only politically equal, and political equality alone could not take them anywhere near the equality dreamed by the philosophers. For that, elimination or at least substantial reduction of economic inequality would also be needed.

Majority decision (in the absence of unanimity) was the basis of democracy from Greco-Roman times. This practice continued in the democratic system that evolved in Europe and America also. However, the old practice of determining majority and minority on headcount basis lost its relevance with the formation of political parties and government formation by the party commanding majority in parliament. Opinion of the ruling party (single party or a coalition of 'likeminded' parties) was assumed to be the opinion of the majority, and headcount, when any legislation was put to vote, became a mere formality since opposition, if any, would be only from a minority outside the ruling party.

This modified idea introduced a new principle – discussion of proposals in party forums before they came up for legislation in parliament. What was approved in these bodies unanimously or on majority basis alone would come up in parliament in the form of bills for legislation. This practice came to be known as 'inner-party democracy'.

Formation of political parties and government formation on party basis, an innovation in the democratic experiment, led to a mushrooming of political parties in countries following the democratic system that evolved in Europe and America. They sprouted under different enticing political labels, but in reality were nothing but the reflection of different and often conflicting interests based on wealth, ideology, religion, ethnicity, community or language. The democratic concept which believed in pluralism and freedom of belief and expression could not prevent their entry into political life. While many of these political parties would not be able to rise to a commanding position and attempt government formation, they could make their presence felt in the event of a tie between major parties and coalition government becoming a necessity.

This development would lead to unhealthy political practices. The primary concern of each party being self-preservation, political parties would stoop to any level while pursuing this goal -- create enemies all around, real or imaginary, and play on ultra-nationalism, patriotism, chauvinism or religious sentiment to divert attention of people from real issues facing them; give false promises to cross over electoral hurdles, and conveniently forget them once they come to power; amass wealth while in power by methods fair or foul, and indulge in bribery and corruption to weaken opposing political parties. Nobody would think of the damage being done to the country as a whole by these unscrupulous methods.

Economic liberalism and individual freedom fostered by the democratic institutions of Europe and America encouraged the growth of capitalism. What capitalism needed was least interference (*laissez-faire*) from government and favourable legislation in matters of taxation. Successive governments that came up, no matter what symbols they wore, obliged and, in return, reaped financial benefits from entrepreneurs. Thus began the unholy nexus between business and ruling dispensations in countries that followed the democratic system. A stage came when governments became lapdogs of corporate giants.

Thus, democracy became a farce – Elected representatives while doing everything for capitalists to flourish, did practically nothing for the welfare of the large number of people who voted them to power. Corporate-controlled media successfully concealed the miseries of people at lower levels in these countries and painted a rosy picture of democracy as the institution that acted as the guarantor of 'freedom' to everyone!

Single-party system with inner-party democracy came out as an alternative to this corrupt form of democracy based on multi-party system. Government formed under the single-party system could feel secure, and there would be no necessity to resort to unhealthy practices for survival. It could move forward with decisions taken within the party on majority basis for the welfare of the country as a whole without hesitation and without indulging in demagogy or populist rhetoric.

Systems which do not exactly fit in with the pattern of the 'democratic' system followed by Western countries are termed 'undemocratic' or 'totalitarian'. According to this classification, even countries which followed the single-party system, considering it as true democracy, would become 'totalitarian'. Limitations imposed on individual freedom to serve social justice would be projected as 'slavery' in those countries.

Dictatorship implies imposition of the will of an individual or a group over others. Tendency towards dictatorship appeared in several ways during the course of social evolution. To begin with, it was the method of tribal chieftains who assumed dictatorial powers and used them for autocratic rule within the tribe. This trend continued with monarchs and reached its final form at the empire stage. Another form was that of one group over others. At the tribal stage, a tribe conquering another tribe collectively imposed its will over the conquered tribe. This trend continued with some groups formed on ethnic, religious or regional basis dominating other similar groups. A third variety was that of an individual, usually a military chief, overthrowing a legitimate government, usurping political power and imposing despotic rule over people with the help of the army. This form, which started at the early stages of social evolution, has continued ever since without any change. A government organised on single-party basis or a government limiting individual freedom to ensure social justice cannot be blindly termed autocratic or dictatorial if it is otherwise following democratic norms in governance.

Overview

As a political institution, democracy originated in Greece in the sixth century BC. The idea spread to Rome and was adopted by the Romans with modifications. Historical evidence points out that a similar experiment was attempted in India too. This political experiment was, however, given up by the beginning of the Christian era, and ancient civilisations moved forward with monarchical institutions.

Democracy of Greco-Roman times was limited in scope as it covered only the upper echelons of society. Large number of people including women could not participate in it. It was an attempt by the aristocrats to share political power exclusively held by monarchs earlier. Philosophers like Plato who lived during this period were not in favour of this experiment. The Greek experiment ended with the Roman conquest of Greece, and the Roman experiment ended when Augustus Caesar replaced it with absolute monarchy. With the disappearance of village republics around the first century BC, the democratic experiment ended in India too.

The idea revived in Europe during the Renaissance Age. Starting from the middle of the seventeenth century, democracy was put on trial once again, and during the last four hundred years it has evolved and matured with improvements and modifications on the original Greco-Roman model to become what it is today. At every stage of its development, there had been attempts to hijack the institution and shape it to serve vested interests. It is by overcoming such negative forces that the institution has reached the shape we see today. It is still not fully free from such threats.

Eighteenth-century philosophers felt that overall development of the individual was a prerequisite for human progress, and for this development, constraints on individual freedom should be removed. Equally important was equality before law. These requirements were codified as enforceable human rights in the legal systems of countries organised on democratic lines. It did not take much time for political observers to realise that individual freedom could not be unlimited, and where it clashed with social freedom, it had to be subordinated to social freedom. They also realised that equality before law could bring only political equality, and in the face of glaring economic inequality, political equality would be inconsequential.

Curtailment of individual freedom where it clashes with social freedom and elimination or reduction of economic inequality would be the new challenges for democracy if it had to move closer to its desired goal of becoming a real 'people's government'. As economic inequality gets eliminated or reduced, conflicting interests resting on inequality will lose their sharpness, and political parties which thrive on such interests will lose their relevance. Election of representatives for legislatures will then be on merit basis, not on party considerations. This will be the visible change that can be looked forward to in the days to come.

Marxism: An Outdated Philosophy?

It has become a fashion these days to reject Marxism as an outdated philosophy. If these 'anti-Marxists' are asked to point out shortcomings in this philosophy, nine out of ten will not be able to give a rational answer, as their opinion is based more on prejudices and misconceptions than on detailed knowledge of the philosophy.

There can be honest criticisms also from those who have studied the philosophy. Such criticisms deserve serious consideration as they will be helpful in deciding the continued relevance of this philosophy.

An important point to be borne in mind is that no philosophy can be considered an absolute or all-time truth. Philosophies represent human thought or collective wisdom which is influenced by time, place and circumstances to a great extent. Even the scriptures which are assumed to be God's revelations are not free from infirmities. Relevance of a philosophy is dependent on the values it projects, values which are useful in shaping our future on more organised lines.

It is not as though a person called Karl Marx suddenly descended from nowhere and rattled out what we call the Marxist philosophy and disappeared. Any person who has correctly understood Marx knows that he was only a sensitive thinker of his time who spent his whole life analysing problems faced by contemporary society, critically examining what other people thought and said about them and formulating his own ideas for the solution of those problems. What he said appealed to many thinkers, and that is the reason for its acceptance as a valid thought. Marx himself would not have expected that what he said would be taken as a dogma or an unimpeachable truth.

Life and Times of Karl Marx

Karl Marx was born in 1818 in a middle-class Jewish family in Trier, Prussia. After his school education in Trier, he studied law at the Universities of Bonn and Berlin and took a doctorate in Philosophy from the University of Jena in 1841.

During his university days, he came in contact with the ideas of the German philosopher George Wilhelm Friedrich Hegel (1770-1831). Hegel's principal achievement was the development of a distinctive articulation of idealism. Modern philosophy, culture and society seemed to Hegel fraught with contradictions and tensions. His aim was to analyse and interpret them as part of a comprehensive, evolving rational unity. According to him, the main characteristic of this unity was that it evolved through and manifested itself in contradiction and negation which led to further development until a rational unity was reached that preserved the contradictions as phases and sub-phases by lifting them to a higher unity.

Hegel emphasised the idealist observation that human experience was dependent on mind's perceptions. Marx disagreed with Hegel's metaphysical assumptions. For him, it was the material world that shaped socio-economic interactions. However, the Hegelian dialectic on changes through contradiction, negation and unity appealed to him, and its influence can be seen in the ideas developed by him on socio-economic changes.

After taking his doctorate, Marx looked for an academic career. But his association with the 'young Hegelians' during his university days proved to be a disqualification in the face of growing government opposition to the Hegelian movement. He, therefore, turned to journalism. Moving to Cologne in 1842, he began his journalistic career as the editor of the radical German newspaper *Rheinche Zeitung.*

Radical opinion propagated by him through this newspaper brought him under government scanner. He was expelled from Germany, and he had to seek refuge in France. There also he suffered the same fate, and had to move to Belgium where he stayed for three years from 1845. When the 1848 Revolution began, he was expelled from Belgium, and he had to relocate to England. He stayed in England till his death in 1883.

The philosophy propounded by Karl Marx was in fact a joint effort, the other brain behind it being that of Friedrich Engels.

Engels was born in 1820 in Barmen, Prussia as the son of a cotton textile manufacturer. He attended secondary school at Barmen. He had to leave his studies before graduation as his father wanted him to pursue a business career. He took up job as an apprentice in a business house in Bremen.

In 1841, he joined the Prussian Army for a one-year compulsory military course and was assigned to Berlin where he attended lectures at the University of Berlin. During his Berlin days, he came in contact with the Young Hegelians. Some articles he wrote during this period were published in the newspaper edited by Marx.

In 1842, he proceeded to Manchester (England) to work in the cotton textile mill partnered by his father. On his way, he stopped at Cologne and met Marx. That was the first meeting between them, and it was quite formal.

While in England, Engels moved around in the industrial area of Manchester and took note of its horrors, notably child labour, overworked and undernourished workers and appalling living conditions. He wrote some articles narrating these conditions and sent them for publication in the newspaper edited by Marx. Observations contained in these articles were later brought out in his influential first book, *The Conditions of the Working Class in England.*

In 1844, Engels decided to return to Prussia. On his way, he stopped to meet Marx who was at that time in Paris after his expulsion from Germany. Marx had read the articles written by Engels and was greatly impressed by them. Particularly impressive was the question posed by Engels: 'A class which bears all the disadvantages of the social order without enjoying its advantages ...... Who can demand that such a class respect this social order?' Marx adopted the idea projected by Engels in those articles that the working class would lead the revolution that would change this intolerable social order.

Engels extended his stay in Paris to help Marx bring out his book *The Holy Family*, a critique on the Young Hegelians. It contained sarcastic remarks against a section of the Hegelians who talked about 'a critical renovation of Christianity'. Marx also pointed out the false notions prevalent under capitalism and said that property, capital, money, wage labour and the like were not figments of imagination but very real. The book made something of a splash in the newspapers. Conservatives lost no time in recognising the radical approach in many of the arguments advanced by the author. It was the first joint effort by Marx and Engels. It also marked the beginning of a lifelong friendship between them.

In 1845, Marx left Paris in compliance with the expulsion order and proceeded to Brussels (Belgium). Engels joined him about two months later, and together they began their journalistic and political activities. It was during their stay in Brussels that Marx brought out his book *The German Ideology* in collaboration with Engels. In this work, Marx parted company with other socialist thinkers of the time whose ideas were still based on idealism, and brought out his philosophy of materialism. This work, which is seen as the best treatment of the concept of 'historical materialism' (historical materialism is basically a theory according to which material conditions of a society's mode of production determined the organisation and development of that society) could not be published during Marx's lifetime as it did not pass censorship. It came out in print only in 1932.

During their stay in Brussels, Marx and Engels visited England and joined the Communist League (an organisation of German *émigrés*) in London. They utilised their stay in England for establishing contact with the political circles of German *émigrés* and exchanging ideas with them.

While Marx made his way to London after his expulsion from Belgium, Engels moved to Prussia. With the failure of an uprising in Prussia in which he took part, he escaped and went to

Manchester to continue in his old job. Together, they began their activities in England.

Marx and Engels made their presence felt in the Communist League when a dispute arose among its members. Some members began to agitate for an immediate uprising by the working class, saying that once the League initiated this uprising, the entire working class of Europe would rise up spontaneously and join it. Marx and Engels disagreed with this. They felt that such an unplanned uprising would be 'adventurist' and would be nothing short of suicide for the League. It would be easily crushed by the government. Changes in society, they argued, were brought about through a scientific analysis of the economic conditions of society and by moving towards revolution through different stages of social development, not through the call of some overenthusiastic people. Conditions in Europe, according to them, had not reached the stage for a successful revolution, and hence the best option for the League at that time would be to lie low and prepare the working class for the revolution it would be called upon to lead at the right time. The upstarts left the League, and opinion of Marx and Engels prevailed.

In 1859, Marx published his work *A Contribution to the Critique of Political Economy*. The book was an analysis of capitalism and quantity theory of money achieved through a critical examination of the writings of leading exponents of capitalism like Adam Smith and David Ricardo. Marx accepted the labour theory of value advocated by Ricardo and went further to delineate the true relationship between use value and exchange value. The preface to this book contains the first connected account of Marxist theory which states that mode of production conditioned the general process of social, political and intellectual life.

In 1867, the first volume of *Das Capital* (The Capital) was published. In this work, Marx analysed the capitalist method of production and elaborated his labour theory of value. He pointed out the alienation of labour under the capitalist method of production and outlined his conception of surplus value and exploitation of labour which he argued would ultimately lead to a falling rate of profit and the collapse of capitalism. The second and third volumes of the work remained in manuscript form upon which Marx continued to work till the end of his life. Both of them were published by Engels after his death with minor corrections and modifications.

Development of Marxist Philosophy

Modern organised socialist movement may be said to have begun with the publication of the *Manifesto of the Communist Party* in 1848. Marx and Engels were entrusted with the task of writing a Manifesto for the Communist League in 1847. The document they brought out in 1848 became not only the Manifesto of the Communist League but also the backbone of the communist movement all over the world since then.

The Manifesto represented the first attempt to put socialism on a scientific basis shedding the utopian form which characterised it till then. It begins with an elucidation of the materialist concept of history and then goes into details and practical propositions relevant to the working class movement on rational lines. It concludes with a clarion call to workers to unite and fight for their rights.

'The history of all hitherto existing societies is the history of class struggles' is the first assertion. It is the struggle between the oppressed and the oppressor classes like that of slaves and their masters in slave-owning societies or serfs and their landlords in feudal societies in the past. Each time, it ended up in a revolutionary reconstruction of society or in the common ruin of the contending classes.

Modern capitalist society which sprouted from the ruins of feudal society did not do away with class antagonisms. On the other hand, it established new classes, new conditions of oppression and new forms of struggle. Society as a whole was splitting up into two classes directly facing each other -- the *bourgeoisie* (capitalists or owners of the means of social production and employers of modern labour) and the *proletariat* (modern wage labourers with no means of production of their own and reduced to selling their labour power for living). The *bourgeoisie*, through 'constant revolutionising of production and uninterrupted disturbances of all social conditions', emerged as the supreme class in society displacing the powers of feudalism. 'It constantly exploits the *proletariat* for its labour power, creating profit for itself and accumulating capital'. In the process, it would really be digging its own grave. The *proletariat* would inevitably become conscious of its potential and rise to power through revolution overthrowing the *bourgeoisie.*

The Manifesto brings out the term 'communist' in its second section. In the preface to the Manifesto (English edition of 1888), Engels wrote: 'By socialists, in 1847, were understood, on the one hand, adherents of various utopian systems: Owenites in England, Fourierists in France, both of them already reduced to the position of mere sects and gradually dying out; on the other hand, the most multifarious social quacks who, by all manners of tinkering, professed to redress, without any danger to capital and profit, all sorts of social grievances, in both cases, men outside the working class movement looking rather to the 'educated classes' for support. Whatever portion of the working class had become convinced of the insufficiency of mere political revolutions and had proclaimed the necessity of a total social change, that portion called itself communist ….. Thus, socialism was, in 1847, a middle-class movement, communism a working-class movement….'

Aim of the communists, as set out in the second section of the Manifesto, should be the formation of the *proletariat* into a class on the basis of their distinct identity, overthrow of *bourgeoisie* supremacy and conquest of political power. This was merely the expression in general terms of a historical movement, not the invention of a would-be universal reformer. In this movement, the communists would represent the interests of the working class as a whole, independent of all nationalities.

Overthrow of *bourgeoisie* supremacy would naturally result in the elimination or abolition of private ownership of property. Quoting precedents like the abolition of feudal rights on landed property during the French Revolution, the Manifesto considered it a historical necessity. Products of labour appropriated for maintenance and reproduction of human life stood excluded from the concept of property. Criticism that abolition of private ownership would amount to an attack on individual freedom and would lead to universal laziness is brushed aside as irrelevant. In effect, it would mean only a change in ownership, collective ownership replacing individual ownership.

On the basis of the principle that a person's consciousness changes with every change in his or her conditions of material existence, the Manifesto points out that notions of freedom, culture, law, status of women, education and even family relation which are the outgrowth of the *bourgeoisie* mode of production will undergo changes when that mode of production together with the property relation created by it undergoes change.

As a result of the development of commerce, the world market and uniformity in the mode of production, 'national differences and antagonisms between people have begun to diminish'. The Manifesto predicts that supremacy of the proletariat with its international appeal will cause them to diminish further. In proportion as the antagonism between classes within the nation vanishes, hostility of one nation to another will also disappear.

Another important observation that the Manifesto makes is that religious ideas had been modified in the course of historical development. As an example, when European slave-owning societies moved to the feudal stage, pagan beliefs of earlier times were overrun by Christianity. When the feudal stage began giving way to the industrial stage, Christianity began succumbing to rational ideas. Religions existing under the *bourgeoisie* order cannot continue in that form under *proletarian* supremacy.

These principles were to guide the communists while proceeding with the establishment of proletarian supremacy. As initial practical steps to raise the working class to the level of the ruling class, certain short-term measures like state-controlled production, nationalisation of communication and transport, public education, etc are also brought out in the Manifesto. The authors admitted that these steps could not be affected 'except by means of despotic inroads on the rights of property and on the conditions of bourgeoisie production'. When, in the course of development, class distinction disappeared, and production and distribution became concentrated in the hands of a vast association of the whole nation, public power would lose its political character and cease to be an organised power of one class to oppress another.

The role of the communists as they work with other parties is also highlighted in the Manifesto. They should fight for the immediate aim of the working class such as improvement in working conditions, increase in wages, etc but it should be in the context of the working class movement as a whole. They could join hands with other parties representing the working class even if differences existed between them and those parties. Even cooperation with the *bourgeoisie* was not ruled out if such cooperation served their interests. That would mean that they could support any revolutionary movement against the existing socio-political order as their objective could be realised only through the demolition of the existing political and social conditions. However, they should 'never cease to instil into the working class the clearest possible recognition of the hostile antagonism between the *bourgeoisie* and the *proletariat*'.

Ideas contained in the Manifesto became the basic principles for the Marxian brand of socialism or communism. Marx and Engels continued to work on them and elaborate them till the end of their life to make them as practical and realistic as possible.

Nothing is permanent; everything changes. This principle governs Marxist thinking. Analysis of socio-economic changes on the above basis convinced Marx and Engels that capitalism was a passing phase in the social evolution. As a socio-economic institution, capitalism emerged after the sixteenth century replacing feudal institutions which oversaw life and activities of people during the Middle Ages. For nearly four hundred years, it dominated the socio-economic life of people. It revolutionised methods of production and enhanced production capability. As with any other institution, capitalism will also fade out in course of time giving way to a new institution capable of tackling problems left unsolved by capitalism such as distribution of wealth. And that new stage was named the socialist stage.

The Manifesto did not produce any immediate spectacular influence on the course of events. However, it succeeded in projecting for the first time an international identity for the working class based on common economic interests cutting across national, ethnic, religious and linguistic barriers.

The Manifesto came out in print in 1848. Within a year of its publication, it was banned, and for the next twenty years it fell into obscurity. The authors felt a revival in fortune in the 1870s. Thereafter, thousands of copies in different languages came out, and communist movements all over the world began to look to it as their guideline.

Lessons from the Paris Commune Experiment

Marxist ideas did not influence the revolution of 1848 or the establishment of The Paris Commune in 1871. The 1848 Revolution was in fact the concluding episode in the struggle to establish *bourgeoisie* supremacy, not a socialist revolution, and ideas contained in the Manifesto had no part in it. Other streams of socialist thoughts were also in circulation at the time when Marx and Engels brought out their socialist ideas. It was the ideas of socialist thinkers like Pierre Proudhon, Mikhail Bakunin and Louis Blanc that guided the organisation and programmes of The Paris Commune. The outcome of The Paris

Commune experiment, however, had considerable influence on the development of Marxist ideology.

Pierre Joseph Proudhon (1809-65) was the founder of the philosophy of 'anarchism', a philosophy considered as 'socialist' by scholars. The word 'anarchy' denotes a state of lawlessness or political disorder according to definition or dictionary meaning. But Proudhon's anarchism meant a society with, as far as possible, no central government and with a great deal of individual freedom. The anarchist ideal was a commonwealth based on altruism, solidarity and voluntary respect for other people's rights. Production, distribution, and exchange of utilities would be done on a cooperative basis without any profit motive. This philosophy rejected both the authoritarian and utopian variants of socialism and believed that human society was steadily moving towards the 'stateless stage' through peaceful reforms and cooperation.

Economic contradictions, according to him, arose mainly from the division of labour, use of machinery for production of utilities, competition and taxation system. He criticised other socialist thinkers who applied their minds to these issues for their incorrect appreciation of facts as well as their palliatives. But he had no solution of his own. 'Instead of offering *a-priori* arguments as solutions', he wrote, 'I shall interrogate political economy as the depository of the secret thoughts of humanity; I shall cause it to disclose facts in the order of their occurrence and shall relate their testimony without intermingling it with my own'.

These ideas were brought out in his book *Philosophy of Poverty* published in 1846. As a rejoinder, Marx came out with his book *Poverty of Philosophy* and criticised Proudhon for his interpretation of human history mixing metaphysics and materialism and for his erroneous application of Hegelian dialectic in the analysis of political economy. He also pointed out fallacies in Proudhon's arguments relating to value.

Like Proudhon, Marx also envisaged a 'stateless' society at the socialist stage, but while Proudhon believed that this stage would be reached through peaceful reforms and cooperation, Marx's finding was that the coercive power of the state would vanish only when class distinctions were wiped out, and this might need some 'despotic inroads' into the rights of property and conditions of bourgeoisie production.

Mikhail Alexandrowich Bakunin (1814-76) was the author of what came to be known as 'collective anarchism'. During his association with Proudhon in Paris, Bakunin imbibed Proudhon's anarchist ideas and, based on them, developed his philosophy of collective anarchism.

He rejected statist and hierarchical systems of power in every name and shape. 'The liberty of man', he wrote, 'consists solely in this that he obeys laws of nature because he himself has recognised them as such and not because they have been imposed upon him externally by any foreign will whatsoever, human or divine, collective or individual'. He rejected the notion of any privileged position or class since social and economic inequality implied by class systems was incompatible with individual freedom. While he accepted elements of Marx's class analysis and theories regarding capitalism, he believed that Marx's method was authoritarian, and his 'dictatorship of the proletariat' would appear more dangerous than Tsarist autocracy.

Religion, according to Bakunin, originated from human ability to think abstractly and fantasise. It is sustained by indoctrination and conformism. Another factor in the survival of religion was the existence of poverty, suffering and exploitation in real life for which religion promised salvation in the afterlife. Oppressors took advantage of religion because many religious people would reconcile themselves with injustice on earth for the promise of happiness in heaven. Religious dogmas were made to appear as divine revelations which ordinary human beings were not expected to question. These dogmas provided the authority for the oppressors to exploit the gullible poor.

In his book *God and the State*, Bakunin argues that 'the idea of God implies the abdication of human reason and justice; it is the most decisive negation of human liberty and necessarily ends up in the enslavement of mankind, in theory and practice'. He reversed Voltaire's famous aphorism that 'if God did not exist, it would be necessary to invent him' by stating that 'if God really existed, it would be necessary to abolish him'.

Ideas of Marx and Engels on religion and God ran parallel to those of Bakunin without going into extremes. 'Religion is the sigh of the oppressed creature, the heart of a heartless world and the soul of soulless conditions. It is the opium of the people .... The criticism of religion is, therefore, in embryo, the criticism of that vale of tears of which religion is the halo....' These were Marx's observations on religion as recorded in his work *A Contribution to the Critique of Hegel's Philosophy of Right*. Marx did not go into the existence or non-existence of God, but the concept of God could have no place in the materialist philosophy developed by him.

Engels went a step further. According to him, 'to primitive man, the forces of nature were something alien, mysterious and superior'. At a certain stage, through which all civilised people passed, he assimilated them by means of personification. It was the urge to personify that created Gods everywhere. Religion was 'nothing but the fantastic reflection in men's minds of those external forces which control their daily life, a reflection in which the terrestrial forces assume the form of supernatural forces'.

From such observations crystalised the Marxist line of thinking on God and religion. The entire natural world is governed by law and absolutely excludes the intervention or action from without. In the evolutionary conception of the universe, there is no room for either a creator or a ruler. We have still not developed any means to confirm or deny the existence of God, and till we are able to decide either way, the concept of God will remain in the realm of speculation. Organised religions came up at a definite stage in the social evolution, and, like any other manmade institution, religion also will lose its relevance when conditions fostering it lose their relevance. There is no condemnation of religion or demand for abolition of God in the Bakunin fashion.

Bakunin wanted workers and peasants to be organised from below in the 'syndicalist' manner (syndicalism was the term used to denote the economic system considered as a replacement for capitalism. It suggested organisation of industries in the form of confederations or syndicates with management by workers). Trade unions would provide the means to defend and improve workers' conditions, and the syndicalist unions would organise occupations and democratic structures through which workplaces would be self-managed and the larger economy coordinated. Marxist thinking was on different lines. Not only industries but the entire state would be under the management of the working class during the transition period. The stateless stage envisaged by Bakunin would be possible only after crossing the transition stage.

Bakunin's socialism sought confirmation of political equality with economic equality. This did not mean the obliteration of natural individual differences. It meant only the creation of equal opportunity for every individual. Marx and Engels also thought along similar lines.

The goal, that is, the evolution of a free, egalitarian society without social classes and government, was common for both Marx and Bakunin. Bakunin believed that this classless, stateless society would be established by the direct action of the masses, while Marx and Engels envisaged the route through the intermediate stage termed 'dictatorship of the proletariat'. Bakunin's argument was that no dictatorship could have any aim other than self-preservation, and it could only beget slavery. For Marx and Engels, it was a practical necessity, and even if it exhibited characteristics of a *bourgeoisie* state, it had to be tolerated. It would lose its relevance progressively as society advanced to socialism.

Lois Blanc, another person whose ideas influenced the working of the Commune, could also be considered a 'socialist', because he believed in the 'just distribution of wealth'. He was not impressed by people who professed themselves to be socialists on philosophical basis. He did not believe in the Marxist idea of a preponderant role for the working class in the revolution that would bring about the 'just distribution of wealth' of his dreams. In fact, he did not believe in popular movements at all.

According to him, a revolution must be the work of a 'handful of determined persons'. They should establish a temporary dictatorship by force. This period of 'transitional tyranny' should be used to disarm the bourgeoisie, confiscate the wealth of the Church and the large property holders and bring commercial and industrial enterprises under state control. Next stage should be the establishment of industrial and agricultural production associations. Once the foundation for the new social order was laid, power could be handed back to the people. He was more concerned with the revolution itself than the imagined future society.

Marx and Engels apparently had nothing to comment on Blanc's ideas, as their approach to establishing the socialist stage was more or less the same. The noticeable feature in Blanc's programme was the cadre-based organisation of men for the revolution. That became an accepted method for organising socialist movements thereafter.

The Paris Commune, established by radical socialists of Paris in 1871, was the first experiment to organise a regime based on socialist principles. Following the defeat and surrender of Emperor Napoleon III in the Franco-Prussian War of 1870, republican and radical deputies of the National Assembly proclaimed France a republic and formed a Government of National Defence. In the election held by this government in 1871, Adolph Thiers was elected the chief executive.

Although the Emperor surrendered, the war went on for some more time. During this period, Prussian troops marched to Paris and besieged the city. Since major part of the regular troops was engaged in the front, the remaining regular and para-military forces in the city were unable to force the Prussians to lift the siege. The city was on the brink of famine, and no help was coming from anywhere. Left with no other alternative, the newly established National Government decided to surrender, accepting the terms dictated by the Prussians.

The National Guard defending Paris was dominated by radical lower-level people of Paris. They were outraged by the peace accord, victory parade conducted by the Prussians in Paris and stoppage of their salary after the war. When Thiers, who formed his government at Versailles, visited Paris, he found the city in the grip of a revolutionary fever. He gave orders to disarm the National Guard thinking that arms in the hands of rebels posed a threat to his government. In the process of disarming, regulars and the National Guard clashed. Thiers escaped and ordered withdrawal of the regulars stationed in Paris. His plan was to come back with a fully trained and equipped force to face the rebels.

When regulars left, the rebels occupied official buildings, raised their socialist flags over them and formed their government in March 1871. This government was known as the 'Paris Commune.' Elections were conducted, and ninety-two deputies, mostly from the working class of Paris, were elected to the Commune.

Thiers worked quickly, and when his force was ready to move, gave orders to advance and take the city. With no great resistance *en route,* the troop advanced into the city. The Commune had no alternative other than unconditional surrender which it did by the end of April, 1871. The first experiment to form a regime based on socialist principles thus ended in failure.

Although it was a failed experiment, it left an indelible impression in the minds of socialist thinkers who considered it a model for the socialist government of the future. During its short life of less than two months, it initiated several progressive measures, the essential preliminary steps to move on to the stage of socialism. In his work *Civil War in France,* Marx observed that the Commune would 'forever be celebrated as the glorious harbinger of a new society'. For both Marx and Engels, the Commune represented the transitional stage between capitalism and socialism.

The main reason for the collapse of the Commune was the absence of a centralised decision-making authority. This reflected the thinking of Proudhon and Bakunin which underplayed the importance of a central authority during the transition stage. The offensive against Thiers' troops was a half-hearted and directionless affair. Marx felt that the Commune could have saved itself if it had faced the offensive in a more organised manner. That justified Marx's idea of a 'dictatorship' at the transition stage, a necessity to save *proletarian* revolution from *bourgeoisie* onslaught.

Socialism and Internationalism

An international identity for the working class based on common economic interest, cutting across national, linguistic, ethnic and religious barriers, was projected by Marx and Engels for the first time through the Manifesto of 1848. They visualised the disappearance of hostility between nations in proportion to the disappearance of class antagonism within nations. These ideas denoted the recognition that, as nationalism was the support base for capitalism and economic imperialism, internationalism would be the support base for socialism.

To translate this theoretical idea into a practical proposition, socialist delegates from various countries met in London in 1864 and decided to set up an 'International Working Men's Association'. Marx attended this meeting in his individual capacity, and his name was included in the sub-committee appointed to write the organisational programme of the association. This association came to be known as the 'First International'.

The International enrolled socialists from various countries as members, and, when at its peak, it reported a membership of about eight million. As it became functional, influence of Marx and Engels on its working became visible. They tried to make the organisation an instrument for building up a class-conscious international proletariat strong enough to wipe out capitalism from the world.

Due to differences of opinion among the 'socialists', there was conflict in the International right from the beginning. The main difference centred on different visions of socialism and the proposed strategy for the realisation of each vision. Differences led to split and its disbandment at the Philadelphia conference in 1876. Although the International ceased to exist, the socialist parties it founded or adopted survived, weak at first, but growing steadily from strength to strength.

Dissolution of the International was a great setback for the rapidly growing working-class movement, and leading socialists were not prepared to give up the idea because of its failure. In another twelve years, the idea revived, and at the conference held in Paris in 1889, socialist delegates from different countries decided to set up a similar organisation once again, and that took shape as the 'Second International'.

The Second International was based on membership of national parties and trade unions with properly elected leadership and political programmes. It was a loose federation with no mandatory powers, but members recognised it as their highest moral authority. Its executive body, The International Socialist Bureau, was set up in Brussels in 1900. By 1912, it represented the socialist parties of all European countries, the United States,

Canada and Japan, with a voting strength of nearly nine million. Among the notable achievements of the Second International were its 1889 declaration of 1st May of every year as the 'International Workers' Day' (May Day) and 1910 declaration of 8th March of every year as the 'International Women's Day'. It also pursued the international campaign for the eight-hour workday to take it to its fulfilment.

Like the First International, the Second International too had to face problems arising from differences of opinion among delegates. Three different strains of thinking prevailed among them. The first one believed in parliamentary democracy of the *bourgeoisie* pattern and gradual move to socialism through reforms. The second one was the Marxist line of class struggle and inevitability of *proletarian* revolution. The third one was the anarchist line of demolition of the *bourgeoisie* state and direct move to socialism. In the London Conference of 1896, the anarchists were expelled, leaving the other two contenders to sort out their differences.

On colonialism, militarism and international conflict, differences were sharp and irreconcilable. The Marxist faction found colonialism incompatible with socialism and wanted its outright rejection. But for delegates from European countries possessing colonies in Asia and Africa, such an option would go against their 'national interest' and, therefore, they wanted to soft-pedal with it.

Militarism and international conflict assumed great significance, particularly as general opinion began to gain ground that colonial powers were drifting towards war. Involvement of the working class in such a war was the concern of the International. The Marxist faction ruled out participation on the ground that it would lead to workers fighting among themselves and destroying working-class unity. But for others, 'national interest' weighed more than socialist aspirations in this case also. Because of these differences, compromise resolutions passed on these issues by the International in the Stuttgart Conference of 1907 became vague and ineffective.

Evasiveness on such important issues was possible till the war began. When the World War began in 1914, delegates were forced to take a definite stand. Inability of the International to take a definite stand led to its collapse. With the collapse of the International, all efforts to lay the foundation for an international society through working class unity made during the nineteenth century ended in failure.

This failure, however, did not invalidate Marxist thinking on the progressive movement of human society towards the socialist stage, and internationalism becoming the support base for the future political and socio-economic order. It convinced socialist thinkers that the method adopted, namely building internationalism through working-class unity, proved inadequate. The *bourgeoisie*, still powerful, could play on the 'nationalist' and 'patriotic' sentiment of people and nullify the internationalist sentiment that could be instilled in them. The idea of building up internationalism before elimination of the bourgeoisie order had to be given up.

Consolidation of Marxist Thinking in the Nineteenth Century

As European society moved further in the latter half of the nineteenth century, the utopian and anarchist strains in socialist thinking began to recede to the background leaving the Marxist line representing class struggle and revolution and the other trend representing gradual evolution of socialism through reforms as the only competitors in the field. Socialists like August Bebel, Wilhelm Liebknecht and Rosa Luxemburg stood by the Marxist line, while socialists like Ferdinand Lassalle and Eduard Bernstein represented the other group, which came to be designated as 'Social Democrats'.

Ferdinand Lassalle (1825-64) believed that after 1848, the revolutionary phase of socialist movement had come to an end, and only a legal and evolutionary approach could hold hopes of success. '…. I have come to the conviction' he wrote to Engels in 1864, 'that nothing could have a greater future or a more beneficent role than the monarchy if it could only make up its mind to become a social monarchy….' He was thus in favour of a monarchical welfare state. By integrating the working class into political and social life, he hoped to achieve a transition from a bourgeoisie state based on private property to a democratic constitutional state.

With these ideas, he founded the 'General German Workers' Association' in 1863. His call to workers was 'organise yourselves as a general workingmen's association and agitate peacefully but untiringly and ceaselessly for the introduction of universal and direct suffrage in all German provinces'. Lassalle expected that many thousands would join his party but was disappointed to find that it attracted not more than five thousand people. After his death, the party merged with the 'Social Democratic Party' and the combined organisation appeared under the name 'Socialist Workers Party of Germany' in 1875.

Another person who found fault with the Marxist line of thinking was Eduard Bernstein (1850–1932). Although he began as a great admirer of Marx and Engels, he parted company later. Seeing around him a 'capitalist prosperity' in which workers were gaining some advantages, he came to the conclusion that capitalism had created new mechanisms such as trade unions and modified electoral procedures which would pave the way for attainment of socialism through reforms. He published a series of articles questioning the Marxist idea of revolution and capture of power by the working class.

The Social Democrats of Germany had their counterparts in other countries also. They all believed that socialism could be brought in through reforms, not necessarily through the overthrow of the *bourgeoisie* state as advocated by Marx and Engels. Such reforms, according to them, would come through agitation by the working class in a 'peaceful manner' within the framework laid down by the *bourgeoisie* state.

Marxists rejected the ideas of the Social Democrats outright. Rosa Luxemburg (1871-1919), a staunch follower of Marx and Engels, came out with a pamphlet *Social Reform or Revolution* criticising the 'revisionist' approach of the Social Democrats. She wrote that the ideas of the Social Democrats would lead not to the realisation of socialism but only to a reform of capitalism or gaining some petty advantages for the working class. For real move towards socialism, demolition of the bourgeoisie state was a prerequisite, she pointed out.

Those who spoke of socialism through reforms had apparently no clear idea about the transformation of society from the capitalist to the socialist stage. It is only in the Marxist line of thinking that one comes across a rational and coherent exposition of the issues involved in this transformation.

'The state', wrote Engels in his Introduction to *The Civil War in France* (authored by Marx, 1891 edition), 'is nothing but a machine for the oppression of one class by another'. In a capitalist society, the *bourgeoisie* wields this machine for oppression of the *proletariat*. The state will lose its coercive nature only in a socialist society, which is conceived as a classless society.

Parliamentary democracy, the political support base for capitalism, will undergo change as society moves to the socialist stage. Rule by majority and one-person-one-vote are flaunted by the *bourgeoisie* to project this institution as democracy. A closer look will reveal that this aspect gives this institution only a semblance of democracy. Economic inequality makes this institution a farce, since real power rests with the *bourgeoisie* only. Majority based on headcount is a deception. On class basis, the proletariat is in the majority, and hence power should really belong to it. Political parties, in the ultimate analysis, represent conflicting class interests. They can have no place in the democracy of a socialist society.

Socialism implies social ownership of the means of production. Changeover to the socialist stage will involve private ownership being replaced by public or social ownership. It is unthinkable that the *bourgeoisie* owning property rights will give it up willingly. That is the reason for the Marxist thinking in terms of 'despotic inroads' into property rights and demolition of the bourgeoisie state as a historical necessity in the move towards the socialist stage. It will be unrealistic to think that anyone can bring in socialism while remaining within the framework of the *bourgeoisie* state.

Attitude of the working class will have to change when society moves to the socialist stage. In a capitalist society, workers work to fill the coffers of the capitalists, selling their labour power at values lower than its real value. They may have to organise themselves and demand their rights even by resorting to agitations if necessary in a capitalist society. But in a socialist society, workers work for themselves, and there will be no exploitation by anyone. In such a situation, agitations will become unnecessary. Any dispute between workers and management will have to be sorted out through arbitration.

God and religion dominated human life from the beginning. They provide an escape route for believers from the world of harsh realities. They are used by the ruling class to keep the oppressed under control. Promise of happiness in an imagined afterlife offered by religion is made use of to make them accept their exploited life as the stepping stone for that imagined happiness. In the materialist philosophy of Marx and Engels, there is no room for a creator or a ruler. They were convinced that rationalism which began from the Renaissance Age would overtake ideas based on faith and belief as human society progressed further, and religion would not be able to continue in a socialist society the way it did in earlier societies.

Socio-economic changes that accompany human society's move to the socialist stage will necessarily induce changes in marriage and family relation. Beginning of the Marxist line of thinking on this issue can be traced to the work *German Ideology* (written by Marx and Engels in 1846) and the Communist Manifesto (1848). Original ideas on this issue were developed further and brought out by Engels in his work *The Origin of the Family, Private Property and the State* (published in 1884).

Anthropologists who had done research on marriage and family relation were unanimous in their opinion that in the beginning, that is, at the hunter-gatherer stage, human beings like other members of the animal species lived a life of sexual promiscuity. Such promiscuity excluded all certainty as regards paternity, and identity at that stage could have been reckoned only through maternity.

Marriage and enforced monogamy for women came up after human beings moved from the hunter-gatherer to the agricultural stage. Marxist line of thinking relates it to change in property relations. As Engels observed, 'monogamy was the first form of family based on the victory of private property over original, naturally developed common ownership'.

Tamed animals and Stone Age implements used for hunting constituted property at the hunter-gatherer stage. At the agricultural stage, non-perishable land became property in addition to the perishable property of the earlier stage. Common ownership at the earlier stage changed to family ownership after the institution of marriage and family took shape. The rule of man in the family (patriarchal system) came up when ownership passed on to the senior male member of the family. Inheritance of property by the biological child of the patriarch was the only aim of monogamy for women.

Enforced monogamy and patriarchal family became the socially accepted norms of civilised life till modern times. Their continuity is attributable to the unchanging property relationship that established itself from the time private ownership replaced the earlier common ownership. The father, the patriarch of the family, exercised unlimited powers over members of the family, and marriage of members became 'an arranged affair' with the bride or groom having no say in the matter.

Institution of marriage and family began to undergo change as society advanced to the stage of capitalism. 'The capitalist mode of production', Engels observed, 'transformed all things into commodities'. It dissolved all ancient relations. Purchase and sale substituted inherited customs and rights. Matrimony began to be looked at as a contract among the capitalist class. The male-dominated patriarchal family began to weaken. However, enforced monogamy continued as before, as private ownership of property and the law of inheritance continued without change.

Conditions of existence dictated a different norm for the property-less *proletariat*. As men and women of this class eked out their living with a meagre return for their labour, economic consideration, as a determining factor in matrimony, would naturally recede to the background. Since property and inheritance did not exist in their case, monogamy, if it existed, would have been only a choice, not a necessity. Patriarchy and male domination could have no social significance at all.

The patriarchal family, as it existed in earlier societies, will lose its relevance as society moves to the socialist stage. Change in property relations will divest the father of his position as the owner of the family property. Together with the elimination of gender-based inequality, the father can, at best, look for respect as a senior member of the family, not for any dictatorial authority over members of the family.

Anxiety about one's own livelihood and the future of children have been important factors which helped enforced monogamy to thrive in capitalist societies. Abolition of the capitalist mode of production along with the property relation created by it will lead to the elimination of economic considerations that stand in the way of free choice. Once they disappear, mutual affection alone will be the guiding force for monogamy. Freedom to choose implies freedom to separate, and partners will be free to terminate their partnership if it does not work satisfactorily. Children will never be a liability as bringing up children would be a social responsibility in a socialist society.

The Social Democrats stressed 'peaceful methods' in realising socialism. That was a contrast to the anarchist approach, which believed in the forcible overthrow of the bourgeoisie state as a prerequisite for realisation of socialism. Marx and Engels also felt that dismantling of bourgeoisie state was a necessity for reconstruction of society on socialist lines, but they did not subscribe to the anarchist philosophy of violence. They were convinced that the proletariat, being in the majority, would be able to 'overwhelm' the *bourgeoisie*, even without the use of force, if it was properly organised and made conscious of its role.

The Social Democrats glossed over the issues mentioned above and carried on with their ideas of evolutionary socialism. Their compromising attitude towards the bourgeoisie alienated them from the working class movement. Like the utopians and the anarchists, they also began to disintegrate by the end of the nineteenth century, leaving the Marxists alone as the trusted representatives of the working class.

Marxism and Revolution in the Twentieth Century

As nineteenth century drew to a close, many began to feel pessimistic about the future of capitalism. Economic depressions and uncertainties of market forces which became a regular feature of the capitalist economy during the latter half of the nineteenth century were mainly responsible for this pessimism. Added to this was the general feeling that capitalist nations of Europe were drifting towards war and self-destruction because of their greed and unhealthy competition for economic monopoly. Many intellectuals began to see Marxism as the only hope to save the world from destruction. This feeling helped to strengthen the socialist movement which was lying dormant after the unsuccessful experiments of the nineteenth century.

According to Marx and Engels, it would be the task of the class-conscious industrial working class to lead the revolution taking society to the stage of socialism. Looking at the progress of capitalism in European countries, they found the conditions in England and France ripe for this revolution. Other countries including Tsarist Russia which were still at the feudal or semi-feudal stage would have to wait, they felt, till these countries advanced on industrial lines. Contrary to their expectation, it was in Russia that a successful 'socialist' revolution took place first.

Russia under the Tsars presented the spectacle of a medieval feudal state. The Tsar, the nobility and the clergy lived in a world of their own, with all the vulgarity and debauchery attached to it, squandering away the wealth of the country for their private life. Outside that world lived the large mass of the exploited and impoverished peasantry. Industrial activity was confined to small areas and was negligible. The impoverished peasantry expressed its resentment through sporadic revolts, but being unorganised, they were easily suppressed by the Tsarist regime.

Marxist influence on Russian revolutionary movement began with the founding of the 'Emancipation of The Labour Group' in Geneva in 1883 by a group of exiled Russian revolutionaries. This group translated Marxist literature into Russian and smuggled it into Russia which helped the educated middle-class to become familiar with Marxist ideology. Soon, small study circles and groups came up popularising this ideology and guiding the resistance movement.

The Russian Social Democratic Labour Party was formed in 1898 to unite revolutionary activities spread over the Russian Empire. The party's programmes were based on Marxist principles. Vladimir Ilyich Ulyanov (better known as Lenin) who became the leader of the Bolshevik Revolution joined this party in 1902.

Lenin was originally in agreement with the Marxist line of thinking that a class-conscious industrial working class was a necessity for the success of proletarian revolution. But seeing the difficulty of implementing this proposition in Russia which was still at the feudal stage, he began to think about some innovation in the Marxist line. He came around to the idea of the Narodniks (revolutionaries who organised resistance movement against Tsarist rule during the latter half of the nineteenth century) that in Russia no revolution can be successful without active participation of the exploited peasantry. That would mean an alliance of the working class and peasants leading the revolution. The improved version of Marxism based on the alliance of workers and peasants came to be known as Marxism-Leninism and became the accepted method to be followed by socialist parties all over the world.

Resentment against the Tsarist government reached its peak by the time the twentieth century began, and it was waiting for a spark to explode. That spark was provided by the Russo-Japanese War of 1904-05 and Russia's humiliating defeat in the War. Soldiers and sailors mutinied. The war caused steep rise in prices and shortage of essential commodities. Workers in St Petersburg went on a strike paralysing normal life in the town. Shooting and killing of people who took part in a hunger march aggravated the situation, and countrywide agitation began.

Finding that the situation was going out of control, the Tsar relented and agreed for reforms. Seriously implemented, the reforms promised by the Tsar would have led to the establishment of a constitutional monarchy in Russia. But the Tsar had no intention to keep up his promise, and once the situation was brought under control, earlier repressive policies continued.

Russia entered the First World War (1914-18) as an ally of Britain and France, and the Tsar himself led his army against the Axis powers. Russian Army suffered reverses after reverses, and the Tsar became thoroughly unpopular. Workers of St Petersburg struck work and organised protest marches. Armed forces stationed in St Petersburg mutinied and joined the workers. Under advice from the Army High Command and ministers, the Tsar abdicated in 1917 handing over power to a 'Provisional Government' headed by Alexander Kerensky.

Kerensky decided to continue Russian participation in the War. Soldiers who believed that peace would return once Tsarist rule ended were disillusioned. They began disobeying orders of superiors and deserting the army in large numbers.

The 'Bolsheviks' (the Marxist faction headed by Lenin) were coming into prominence by this time. Four days before the Tsar's abdication, the Petrograd (St Petersburg) workers had formed a council named 'The Petrograd Soviet', and it was dominated by the Bolsheviks.

In July 1917, a spontaneous demonstration of workers and soldiers began in Petrograd demanding Kerensky's ouster and transfer of power to the Petrograd Soviet. It was peaceful, but the Provisional Government with the support of the 'Mensheviks' (socialist faction other than the Bolsheviks) ordered an attack on the demonstrators. In the confrontation, hundreds of demonstrators were killed. This incident set up a wave of sympathy for the Petrograd workers, and soon, strikes and demonstrations spread to the rest of the country. The Bolsheviks used this opportunity to capture power. In October 1917, the 'Red Guards' (armed factory workers) of Petrograd systematically captured major government facilities, communication installations and vantage points without any opposition. Kerensky gave up and escaped to the United States.

That was the Bolshevik Revolution of 1917. Tsarist rule ended, and Lenin and his team formed a new government. By any standard, it should be considered a peaceful revolution because it took place with very little violence. In Lenin's words, 'the Bolsheviks found power lying in the street and picked it up'. In other words, this revolution did not happen the way one should have thought of the 'Marxist revolution' with its call for workers to unite and overthrow the *bourgeoisie*. It was a mere coincidence that power came into the hands of Marxists. Life in the country continued as usual, in spite of this change.

The topmost priority for the Bolsheviks who captured power after overthrowing the Provisional Government was bringing the war to an end. Leon Trotsky was appointed by Lenin as the Commissar for Foreign Affairs. He arranged a ceasefire and peace talks. The Treaty of Brest-Litovsk, signed in December 1917, drew the curtain over the war between Russia and the Axis Powers.

More than anything else, it was the possibility of a Civil War that forced Lenin to seek peace at any cost. Assumption of power by the Bolsheviks was seen as a threat by landlords, industry owners, military officials and even socialists who supported the Kerensky regime. European powers also saw the rise of Bolshevism as an ideological threat to their governments. The arch-imperialist Winston Churchill wanted Bolshevism to be 'strangled in the cradle'. Supported by foreign powers, the anti-Bolsheviks formed a loose federation known as the 'White Movement' and unleashed a Civil War that lasted for nearly five years.

The young Bolshevik State found it difficult to face this challenge. It lacked organisation and resources. All that Lenin could do was instruct party cadres in each locality to organise themselves into Soviets and defend themselves with whatever they could lay their hands on. Their faith in their leader and ideological motivation provided inspiration for these cadres. These factors were totally lacking in the enemy camp consisting of mercenaries and adventurers. Trotsky was appointed Commissar for war. He organised the Red Guards into a proper fighting force making it the nucleus of the future Red Army. Slowly, the Bolsheviks gained ground and succeeded in bringing the Civil War to an end. The Soviets formed during the Civil War joined together to form the Union of Soviet Socialist Republics.

Russian economy was in shambles as a result of participation in the First World War. Condition became worse still during the Civil War. Trade embargo placed by western nations compounded the problem. A famine occurred in the Volga region during the period 1921-22. No help could be expected from any of the advanced European countries. As a result of these developments, the Bolshevik State had to go in for war-time measures. That included nationalisation of industries, state control of trade, rationing, centralised distribution system and compulsory procurement of food grains etc. These measures continued till the economy gained some stability. Marx and Engels laid down these methods in the Communist Manifesto as the first stage in the move towards socialism. The Soviet Union, however, introduced them more as a necessity to face economic problems created by circumstances than in adherence to Marxist principles.

Experience during the Civil War convinced Soviet leaders that political opponents within the country could be more dangerous than foreign elements during an emergency like the Civil War. This led to their banning of all dissident political parties in the country leaving the Bolshevik party alone to rule without any possibility of its being replaced by any other party.

For parliamentary democracies following multi-party system, this gave a chance to denounce the Soviet Union as a dictatorship. Soviet defence against this accusation was that if democracy meant the rule of majority, the working class, being in the majority on class basis, should have the right to rule. Political parties, in whatever name or form they might appear, in the ultimate analysis, represented conflicting class interests. They had to be eliminated to establish a classless society.

This would appear a convincing argument, but the capitalists would not accept it. For them, their system alone was democracy. And this provided a good weapon for them in their propaganda war against the Soviet Union. But it became an established principle in Marxist thinking and was accepted as a model by all communist governments that came up during the latter half of the twentieth century.

Marx and Engels visualised the proletarian revolution as a world revolution. Call for international workers' unity in the Communist Manifesto was in this context. To a great extent, this seems to have been the view of most Bolshevik leaders before the October Revolution. They were of the opinion that proletarian revolution would not be successful in a single country, however advantageously that country was situated, as it would be impossible for that country to survive in a capitalist environment. Having come to power after the overthrow of Kerensky regime, Stalin and many others were not in favour of giving up power, and were putting forth the argument that it would be better to hold on to power as socialists in power would be in a better position to help revolutionary movements elsewhere and prepare them for the world revolution.

Stalin's ideas prevailed, and the new experiment of establishing socialism country-wise began. The Soviet Union created the Third International in 1919 with the aim of providing assistance to socialist movements outside the Soviet Union. This was an innovation on the Marxist idea of world revolution, and thereafter, communist parties all over the world began working on this basis. Consequently, the stateless society visualised by Marx and Engels would become a distant possibility, as it had to wait till all regions of the world moved on to the stage of socialism independently.

Following Lenin's death in 1924, Stalin took over the leadership. He was aware that if the Soviet Union was to survive, it had to advance technologically and industrially, and 'catch up' with the advanced countries. No assistance could be expected from capitalist countries. Trade embargo placed by them came in the way of export and import of goods. As the country's economy was still not out of the feudal stage, generating surplus capital needed for investment was not easy. In spite of all these problems, he decided to push forward with his plan for the rapid industrialisation of the country.

The biggest problem Stalin faced was on the food front. The urban sector was facing acute shortage of food items. Landlords were hoarding food grains and exploiting shortages in the urban sector. Next was the problem of getting machinery and equipment needed for organising industry and agriculture on modern lines. Then, there was the shortage of trained personnel. Equally important was health and hygiene of people and dwelling places for them. Simultaneous activity on all these fronts needed a carefully drawn-up plan to fix priorities and allocate resources.

Thus began *piatiletka* or five-year plans of the Soviet Union. More than any philosophical consideration, it was practical exigency that drove Stalin to resort to this idea. Although it meant privations, sacrifices and hard work, in expectation of a better tomorrow, workers and peasants responded positively to Stalin's call for greater and greater effort to make the plans successful.

The five-year plans helped the Soviet Union to move forward fast economically and socially. They became a model for socialist regimes that emerged in the latter half of the twentieth century for their rapid socio-economic development. Even leaders who did not believe in Marxist principles found planned economy better for underdeveloped economies in Asia and Africa.

A noticeable feature of Stalin's five-year plans was the absence of space for private capital. This meant state control over the means of production envisaged by Marx and Engels in the Communist Manifesto. It helped the plans to get a philosophical backing.

For the capitalist world, however, it meant something else. It could not reconcile with the idea of private capital being denied its 'rightful' place in economic activity. It, therefore, denounced Stalin as a 'tyrant' and propagated that communism was 'worse than slavery'.

Stalin's defence against the capitalist accusation was that when right to work was guaranteed to workers, it became obligatory for them to work according to the requirement of the state. In a socialist state, workers worked for themselves, and no one exploited them. What was seen in the Soviet Union was socialist discipline, not enslavement. Capitalists who used coercive methods to extract free labour through their 'hire and fire' policy and threat of unemployment had no moral right to accuse the Soviet Union on this count.

Experience convinced socialist thinkers later that while state control and planned economy would be a necessity at the transition stage between capitalism and socialism, controls at the cost of market forces and entrepreneurial skills could prove harmful to economic development in the long run, particularly as the economy grew. They seem to have come around to the view that instead of sticking to the conservative Marxist approach, it would be better, from a practical point of view, to adopt some of the measures which helped the rapid development of capitalism, like entrepreneurship. Liberalisation or relaxation of controls and space for private capital within the socialist framework could also be thought of as part of the strategy for rapid development. This, again, was a modification of original Marxist thinking.

Success of the socialist revolution in Russia inspired socialist thinkers all over the world, and quite a few countries established socialist regimes replacing *bourgeoisie* regimes during the latter half of the twentieth century. Even in countries where no such regime change took place, Marxist ideas began to exercise significant influence on their socio-economic policies. European colonies in Asia and Africa which were struggling for freedom from colonial rule also felt the impact of socialist ideas, and their freedom movements began to incorporate the social element contained in Marxist ideas into their programmes which were purely political till then.

As the socialist experiment progressed, countries involved began to see some unhealthy trends coming out. The idea of socialism country-wise which became the accepted model after it began in the Soviet Union had its own risks. Although all socialist countries went by the principles of Marxism-Leninism as their philosophical foundation, in their practical application in each country, differences cropped up, and these differences led to mutual criticism. In their approach to international problems also, differences came out with 'national interest' taking precedence over 'international brotherhood', the backbone of Marxist philosophy. These differences led to military confrontations between major socialist countries in the 1960s and 1970s, and they had serious repercussions on the socialist movement.

Both the Anarchists and the Marxists were unanimous in their opinion that demolition of the bourgeoisie state was a prerequisite for establishment of socialism. When Bakunin and Marx formulated this idea, overthrow of a ruling dispensation might have been a simple job, possibly a mission to be accomplished by a determined group in a surprise move. Things have changed now with improved communication systems and methods of governance. A government sitting far away can now 'nip in the bud' any revolt being hatched anywhere within its jurisdiction. Even for properly organised guerilla warfare to be successful in its effort to displace an established government, it will be necessary to have external help, and it has to be preferably based outside the state jurisdiction. It can be a prolonged affair too.

In these changed circumstances, the idea of 'overthrow' of an established state, with or without force, came up for a re-look among socialist thinkers. They had to find an alternative, and they came to the conclusion that the only way open would be to come to power through the electoral method followed in *bourgeoisie* democracies. This could be made to fit in with the Marxist idea of 'overwhelming' the *bourgeoisie* without the use of force. Although not very promising, it is now being tried by parties organised on Marxist lines in all countries which are under *bourgeoisie* rule.

Collapse of the Soviet Union and Stagnation in the Socialist Movement

Seeing the progress made by the socialist movement during the middle of the twentieth century, many people believed that capitalism was nearing its end, and socialism was not far away. Those who expected the world to turn socialist in the foreseeable future were in for a rude shock when the Soviet Union collapsed in the 1990s. The episode put socialist thinkers all over the world into an introspective mood. The point they considered was whether it was the failure of Marxist philosophy itself or whether the fault lay in its implementation.

It was difficult for them to find fault with the broad principles enunciated by Marx and Engels. The duo tried to explain socio-economic changes on a scientific basis, and most of their ideas were derived by critiquing the ideas of contemporary scholars. By any standard, these principles represented the advanced thinking of the age.

The central idea of Marxism that nothing is permanent and everything undergoes change, is an incontrovertible truth repeated time and again from the days of Gautama Buddha.

Changeover from capitalism to socialism, visualised by Marx and Engels, was based on this truth. Capitalism was seen as one of the stages in the social evolution. After serving the purpose for which it was created, it would fade out, and a new institution appropriate to the next stage would come up to take its place. That is how human society progressed from the hunter-gatherer to the modern stage. Values, attitudes, and social interactions of the existing stage will undergo changes catering to the needs of the changed institution. This is a powerful idea capable of withstanding any criticism.

Unable to spot any incongruity in the philosophical plane, scholars directed their investigation to the implementation part. Problems faced by the Soviet Union from the October Revolution to the days preceding the collapse and the way those in power handled them came up for critical examination to find out whether there was any lapse anywhere.

Revolutionary reconstruction of society from the ruins of capitalism was left by Marx and Engels to those who would be directly concerned with it. Soviet leaders had nothing to fall back upon for guidance when they embarked on the socialist course and were, therefore, going by *ad hoc* measures while tackling day-to-day problems. Socialism country-wise, planned economy, one-party rule etc. were practical measures dictated by circumstances, and the philosophical justification given was to counter enemy accusations. For other countries embarking on the socialist course, measures adopted by the Soviet Union became precedents.

Economic planning introduced by Stalin helped the country to advance rapidly in the industrial and economic sectors. It is an accepted fact that but for this industrial and economic development during the 1930s, the Soviet Union would have found it difficult to face German onslaught during the Second World War.

The war took a heavy toll on men and materials and pushed the economy back to square one. A disproportionate share of resources had to be allocated to improve defence capability during the war, and that made resources needed for other sectors scarce. Post-war reconstruction put great pressure on the economy. Added to this was the Cold War and encirclement by the United States during the post-war era which prevented the Soviet Union from scaling down its defence expenditure. People responded positively to Stalin's call for greater effort during the 1930s hoping for a better tomorrow. Even after fifty years, that better tomorrow was nowhere in sight. Such a situation was bound to lead to pessimism and even loss of faith in the system itself.

These were problems for which no easy solutions existed. A capable and farsighted leadership alone could have taken the country out of the abyss into which it had fallen. Stalin died in 1953. Following his death, a power struggle erupted in the Soviet hierarchy. Georgy Malenkov who succeeded Stalin was replaced by Nikita Khrushchev. He tried to introduce changes in the economy by laying greater stress on the production of consumer goods. His policy did not make any perceptible change in the overall situation. He was ousted from power in 1964, and Leonid Brezhnev took over. During Brezhnev's tenure, lasting for about eighteen years, no radical measures were initiated, and the economy began to stagnate. Michael Gorbachev who succeeded him initiated his new policy *perestroika* (restructuring), and its attendant radical reforms. It was followed by the policy of openness (*glasnost*). These policies only led to chaos, and, in the process of pursuing them, he unwittingly played into the hands of unscrupulous persons. That led to the collapse of the Soviet Union.

Common people in the Soviet Union had no role in this *coup*. No doubt, they were suffering, but the fact is that they had never seen anything better before, and, therefore, there was nothing to compare with. Under socialist rule, they had a guaranteed livelihood, comprehensive social security at a modest but real level and a socially and economically egalitarian society to live in. If their condition was as bad as that of 1917, they would have been at the forefront of the move to dislodge the Soviet government. They were only mute witnesses to what was happening. Scholars came to the conclusion that responsibility for what happened must squarely rest with the inexperienced and incompetent leadership.

Following the collapse of the Soviet Union, socialist regimes in East Europe collapsed. Seeing this, capitalist saints predicted that other socialist countries would follow the same course. But that did not happen. China, Indochina, North Korea and Cuba which were moving on socialist lines survived, possibly because of the alertness displayed by leadership in those countries.

Socialist movement which was spreading fast all over the world during the latter half of the twentieth century began to show signs of a slowdown or stagnation as the curtain fell over the century. In Indonesia, the Sukarno regime which leaned heavily on the socialists was toppled, and the military regime that came in its place suppressed the Communist Party of Indonesia. In Burma also, the left-oriented government was overthrown in a military coup, and the military rule that followed virtually wiped out socialists. In other Asian, African and Latin American countries where the movement made sufficient progress during the middle of the century, a tendency for slowing down could be noticed.

Divided loyalties following military confrontations between socialist countries and a general lack of revolutionary zeal could be considered the main reason for this setback. Added to this was the determined effort of antisocialist forces backed by the Central Intelligence Agency of the United States to stage a comeback. Economic boom in the capitalist world during the latter half of the century also had a hand in weakening the movement.

Overview

Socialist ideas which originated in the first half of the nineteenth century were placed on rational foundation and made the guideline for the working class movement by Marx and Engels in the middle of the century. After a failed experiment during the latter half of the century, the movement entered the twentieth century with renewed vigour. Its first successful experiment in shaping political and socio-economic institutions on socialist lines began in Russia in 1917. During the next fifty years, the movement grew fast becoming a powerful influence on human thinking. But thereafter it began to slow down or stagnate raising questions about its future.

Marxism is a way of interpreting history – history as a record of class struggle, struggle between the oppressed and oppressor classes like slaves and their masters in slave-owning societies, serfs and their landlords in feudal societies or workers and their employers in capitalist societies. Each time, the struggle ended in a revolutionary reconstruction of society or mutual destruction of the contending classes. Capitalism failed to solve class conflict in society, and the working class, once it becomes conscious of its rights, will overthrow capitalism and establish a classless socialist society.

Everything changes, nothing is permanent. Capitalism came up at a definite stage in the social evolution and established itself dismantling the feudal state. It lifted human society to a higher and more organised stage by revolutionising method of production. Values and social interactions of the earlier stage changed adjusting to the needs of the new institution. It will fade out once it outlives its utility, as a natural historical process, and will give way to a new institution capable of solving problems like abnormalities in the distribution of wealth left unsolved by capitalism. Like earlier ones, the new institution also will have its own values and social interactions different from those of the capitalist stage.

This, in essence, is Marxism. Marx and Engels developed these ideas relying on the findings of scholars like Charles Darwin and Friedrich Hegel and critically examining observations of leading exponents of capitalism like Adam Smith and David Ricardo. They represented the advanced thinking of the age.

Intellectuals who critically examined Marxist philosophy could not find any infirmity in it. Many of them found the Marxist line of thinking rational and the projected move to socialism indisputable. Only the capitalists and their cronies considered Marx and Engels as outdated philosophers and their philosophy obsolete. More than any valid argument, it was survival instinct that stood behind their destructive criticism. In pursuing this objective, they never hesitated to gloss over accepted principles like the evolution theory.

Like all other philosophical concepts, Marxism also had to go through alterations and interpretations when it came to implementation. Marx and Engels considered industrially advanced countries like England and France ripe for the proletarian revolution. However, it was in feudally stagnating Russia that Marxist philosophy began its first successful trial. Lenin felt that for the revolution to be successful in Russia, alliance between the working class and peasants was essential. This was a modification of Marxist thinking which placed its reliance exclusively on the industrial working class for a successful proletarian revolution.

The inexorable tendency of capital to accumulate and become concentrated in ever fewer hands and competition among capitalists leading to diminishing return on capital, observed in contemporary society, provided the basis for Marx and Engels to predict the collapse of capitalism under the weight of its own contradictions. This proved to be an incorrect assumption. Capitalism did not collapse as predicted but managed to survive by expanding beyond national boundaries during the stage of economic imperialism.

Marx and Engels had projected an international identity for the working class cutting across ethnic, linguistic and religious barriers, and had imagined internationalism to be the support base for the socialist society conceived by them. Two attempts to lay the foundations for an international society based on working-class unity made during the nineteenth century ended in failure, differences of opinion and 'nationalist' aspirations coming in the way of international cooperation. Socialist thinkers learned from this experience that working-class unity alone would be insufficient to build up an international society.

They had also imagined the proletarian revolution as a world revolution wiping out capitalism from the surface of the earth in one stroke. This postulate also proved to be somewhat unrealistic. In the debate that followed the assumption of power in Russia by the Bolsheviks, on whether they should give up power and wait for the imagined world revolution or whether they should hold on to power which had come into their hands accidentally, it was decided to go for the latter option. Socialism country-wise became the accepted principle of Marxist ideology thereafter.

Overthrow of the bourgeoisie state was a prerequisite for the establishment of socialist society for both anarchists and Marxists. When this idea was formulated by socialist thinkers in the nineteenth century, this operation would not have been a formidable task. Roadblocks, disruption of communication facilities, etc., by a determined group could bring down a government. But things changed with the development of science and technology. Administrative machinery of a government nowadays is well equipped to 'nip in the bud' any conspiracy against that government being hatched anywhere within its jurisdiction. With the idea of insurrection becoming obsolete, the only chance for the socialists to come to power now is through the *bourgeoisie* electoral method.

In their eagerness to establish a socialist society rapidly, Soviet leaders at the early stage of the socialist experiment in Russia, and Chinese leaders later imitating the Soviet model, moved fast replacing private ownership with social ownership. This move proved to be counterproductive and led to stagnation in economic development. The age-old wisdom of not throwing the baby along with bathwater seems to have dawned on them, and under the changed thinking, private capital and individual entrepreneurship began to be accommodated within limits in the socialist establishment. Socialism began to be looked upon not as a break with the past, but a continuous social process with suitable corrections, where necessary, in the earlier institution.

As an offshoot of this changed thinking, socialist thinkers now explore the possibility of eliminating or reducing economic inequality by narrowing the gap between the rich and the poor through state intervention rather than through extremist measures advocated by earlier socialist thinkers. With the elimination or reduction of economic inequality through the new method and disappearance of discrimination based on gender, race, colour or caste which is also definitely on the way out, human society, according to the new thinking, would be well poised for its move towards socialism.

Marx and Engels did not leave any readymade formula for reconstruction of society after dismantling the *bourgeoisie* state. That task was left to those who would become the architects of the new society. Soviet leaders were virtually groping in the dark when power came into their hands, and most of the measures adopted to shape Russian society on socialist lines were based on *ad hocism* rather than preconceived notions. Whatever be the method they adopted, they were clear in their minds about their aim, that is, the establishment of an egalitarian socialist society. China, too, had to go through similar experiences.

The crusading spirit that gave momentum to the socialist movement noticed at the early stages is what one misses today. While surviving communist regimes are adjusting themselves to changing international environment, Communist parties in countries which are still under *bourgeoisie* rule are struggling for survival, and in this struggle even basic principles stand the risk of being compromised.

For a discerning observer, however, this would appear only as a passing phase. Great religions like Hinduism and Christianity had gone through such experiences. By no means should this lull be interpreted as marking the end of socialist thinking. Radical thinking thrives better when economic conditions deteriorate and life becomes difficult for people. The latter half of the twentieth century witnessed an economic boom for the capitalist world, and the overall prosperity resulting from this boom was one factor which contributed to the dampening of the 'left' fervour.

Latter half of the twentieth century witnessed capitalism reaching its zenith. The United States as the leading capitalist power dominated the world during this period with its military might and money power. The corporate sector in the United States was the biggest beneficiary of this development. Corporate 'giants' grew wealthy beyond imagination. European nations which were pioneers in the development of capitalism were reduced to the status of camp followers to the United States.

This happy situation also would appear equally ephemeral. Economic recession which commenced at the beginning of the present century in the capitalist world and emergence of Asian and African nations as powers to be reckoned with are becoming challenges to the continued prosperity and dominance of the United States. China developing on different ideological lines has now become a close competitor to the United States, and the American reaction to the Chinese challenge betrays a feeling of uncertainty about the future. In the event of China overtaking the United States -- a proposition which has already moved from the probable to the possible stage and is showing signs of moving to the certainty stage in the foreseeable future, capitalism and its support base, the institution of parliamentary democracy, which are heavily dependent on the United States for survival may find themselves in a precarious condition. Dismantling of the *bourgeoisie* state envisaged by Marx and Engels may take place not necessarily in the manner they imagined but through an unexpected turn of history.

Dissolution of the *bourgeoisie* state would initiate a reorganisation of society. In the past, such reorganisations led to rectification of shortcomings of the earlier stage and lifting of society to a higher stage in the social evolution. We should expect such a historical move in future reorganisations also.

While capitalism revolutionised the method of production and increased productivity, it failed to bring about a just distribution of wealth. Economic inequality and widening gap between the rich and the poor that resulted from this shortcoming are the main causes of political instability seen in the world these days, and political instability threatens peaceful life. For a better and more organised existence, this abnormality will have to be addressed during the reorganisation.

With the reduction in economic inequality, class composition of society can be expected to undergo drastic changes. Democratic institutions will have to reorient themselves to cater to this change. Multi-party system of present-day representative democracy based on conflicting class interests may lose its relevance.

Along with this change, discrimination based on sex, caste, creed or colour which is directly or indirectly related to economic inequality and which does not fit in with the democratic way of life also can be expected to vanish.

Rational ideas replacing ideas based on faith and belief and religion losing hold on people would be other noticeable features of the reorganised stage. Religions exercised a profound influence on human beings from the beginning. During the capitalist stage, religions and ideas based on faith and belief began succumbing to rational ideas. At the reorganised stage in which rationalism is likely to dominate human thinking, ideas based on faith and belief will cease to exercise any perceptible influence on society.

Another area to be affected by the change will be family relations. Male-dominated families with enforced monogamy for women became the socially accepted norm for all civilised societies ever since human society moved from the hunter-gatherer to the agricultural stage. The senior male member of the family became the owner of family property, and other members had to depend on him for their livelihood. As family members began to earn their livelihood independently, their dependence on the head of the family for livelihood was reduced. In the reorganised stage, property relations will undergo change, and consequently, the senior male member will lose his position of dominance as he will no longer be the owner of the property. As women gain equality, enforced monogamy will lose its support base, and marriage may take the form of a contract terminable by either party if it does not work satisfactorily.

For a sensible observer analysing socio-economic changes on rational basis, this would be the shape of society at the next stage in the social evolution. And that was exactly what Marx and Engels visualised a hundred and seventy years ago. Therein lies the continued relevance of Marxism.

Part II

RECOLLECTIONS

Lakshmi and Her Small World

The village where I spent my childhood days had changed beyond recognition when I saw it again twenty-five years later. Gulf money had transformed it. The only recognisable landmark I could see was the banyan tree and the patch of land surrounding it where children used to play during their holidays. A superstition that a *yakshi* (vampire or fairy, in English) resided on top of that tree and mishaps would sweep the village if that tree was cut down saved that magnificent tree from destruction.

When boys of my age group were not available to play with me, I used to seek the partnership of Lakshmi, a girl slightly younger to me in age and staying in my neighbourhood. She was not fond of marbles, running race or hide-and-seek but preferred the husband-wife game. According to her, the husband worked in the field while the wife cooked food in the kitchen. At mealtime, the wife fed her husband and children and ate whatever was left. In the evening, the husband would invariably visit the village tavern to 'refresh' himself and, if he had 'a drink too many', would fight with his wife for no rhyme or reason. The wife should know how to put up with it because that is how a dutiful wife should behave. This was the husband-wife game which her background had taught her at that tender age. I would act well as the husband under her able direction, and I used to enjoy the role of the tipsy husband.

Poetry was emotion recollected in tranquillity for the English poet William Wordsworth. Like other human beings I too become emotional at times, especially when I recollect some of my childhood experiences, but my emotion does not transform into poetry for the simple reason that I lack the poetic instinct.

Standing by the side of that banyan tree and going down memory lane, I could see the whole drama enacted once again. What a wonderful experience it was! I could not help laughing at the fantastic world in which we lived as children. When the curtain fell, the world of realities came back. I started thinking about my childhood friend Lakshmi. She must have married and settled somewhere. I may not be able to see her again in life.

While trekking back home through the soporific countryside, I came across an elderly man, possibly a native of that village, whose appearance gave the impression that he was slow in catching up with the changing times. A smiling face from me was sufficient for him, in his typical village fashion, to enter into a discourse with me. Most of what he said amounted to criticism of the younger generation or expression of distress at what appeared to him as falling standards compared to the glorious times of his younger days.

It did not take much time for me to fish out from his detailed knowledge of the people in the locality that Kunjan Kutty, Lakshmi's father, died a few years back, and her mother Kunjathi had become insane. Her younger brother, Narayanan, fell into bad ways, left the village six or seven years back and was never heard of again. Lakshmi got married when she was thirteen years old, and her husband died two years after the marriage. A second marriage after a gap of about three years proved disastrous. Her husband became a drunkard. She lived about two kilometres away from that village. A few more casual questions, and I could make out her approximate location.

Next day I set out to meet Lakshmi. A dilapidated hut was her small world. A grey-haired old lady was sitting in one corner of the veranda and pouring out incoherently whatever came to her mind. Although I recognised her, she showed no sign of recognising me, and, knowing her mental state, I did not bother to introduce myself. Peeping through the window, Lakshmi saw me and appeared at the door, showing her face partly, to enquire who I was and what I wanted. She bore no resemblance to the image I had of her in my mind. Signs of premature ageing were deeply embedded in her face.

'Don't you recognise me? I am Balan, your old playmate'. That statement was met with a faint smile and a blank look which suggested to me that she was lost in thought for a while. Thoughts of a happier past can sometimes make an unhappy present more painful.

I was at a loss as to how to proceed further. She brought a rickety chair from inside and, placing it on the veranda, requested me to take my seat. I agreed and sat down. Having heard the previous evening that her married life was a failure, I deliberately avoided asking questions about her husband. 'Children must have gone to school' I started, trying to end the silence. A negative facial expression was the reply, and that conveyed to me that she had no children.

Before I could proceed further, a shabbily dressed clumsy fellow with dishevelled hair and unshaven face crossed the gate and came towards the house, pouring abuses at everything and everybody. His zigzag walking and irrelevant talk were clear expressions of his drunken state. I could make out that it was her husband. Seeing him approaching, Lakshmi quickly withdrew to a safer place inside the house. Without taking note of me, he broke into the house with the choicest of abuses for her, even suspecting her fidelity. He came out the same way he went in and appeared to be leaving the house. Stopping short of the gate and turning round, he shouted: 'Looks like a big catch….I will be back…. keep my share…will have one more drink'. I felt like pouncing on him and thrashing him, but thinking that it might create more problems for Lakshmi, I controlled my temper.

When he went out, Lakshmi appeared again at the door with the same composed face. No further question or explanation was needed. I got up to say good bye and asked her whether I could be of any help to her. A polite decline was the response. Her sense of pride and self-respect would not permit her to bow down before anyone even if she had to go through the worst of privations and humiliations in life. It was an eye-opener for me.

Lakshmi's image remained stuck in my mind for quite some time. Her life seemed to me a miserable existence without any hope or expectation. 'When winter comes, can spring be far behind?' asks the English poet Shelly in his *Ode to the west Wind*. Well, Mister Shelly, for a person like Lakshmi, winter can go on without an end in sight, and spring may remain a mirage.

An Hour in the Sky Between Life and Death

When the first India-Pakistan War broke out in September 1965, my Regiment, located at that time in the southern region of the country, was moved to the front and deployed in an operational area in the north-western sector. Three days later, operational requirements necessitated pulling out one Battery from that area for deployment in the Rajasthan sector. Because of the emergency, one troop was to be airlifted while the remainder of the Battery was to be moved by rail. I was detailed as the officer in charge of the troop to be airlifted.

Men, weapons, vehicles, and stores to be airlifted were pulled out during night from the area where they were deployed and concentrated in the camouflaged parking area of the airfield by dawn. Two Air Force transport aircraft (Fairchild Packets), each making three trips, were to ferry men and materials to the destination. I was to proceed in the first aircraft, and my second-in-command, a Junior Commissioned Officer (JCO), was to come in the last trip after making sure that nothing belonging to the troop was left behind.

The pilots and crew assembled at dot seven in the morning. I approached the pilot of the aircraft in which I was to fly and greeted him in the usual service manner. From the name plate he wore on his chest, I could make out that he was a Keralite, and that was sufficient to create some familiarity dispelling the professional aloofness normally seen anywhere. Within half an hour, weapons and materials were loaded, and men boarded the aircraft. The pilot started the engines and, after getting clearance from the Air Traffic Control (ATC) on the radio, taxied the aircraft to the take-off point. When permission was granted for take-off, the engines roared, and within minutes we were airborne.

I expected the aircraft to climb straight and disappear into the clouds in no time. But that was not happening. Instead, I could see clearly through the window pane people and vehicles moving on the roads below suggesting that the aircraft must be flying at an altitude not more than a thousand feet. I asked the pilot why he was flying low. He smiled and said: 'We are flying close to the enemy border. If we go beyond this altitude, there is the possibility of our aircraft being picked up by enemy radars, and that would mean a sure scramble. We will, therefore, have to continue like this for about an hour'. 'Is not low-flying risky?' I interjected with my layman's understanding. 'No doubt it is. But then, going up is also equally risky', said the pilot. And then he smilingly asked: 'Which one do you prefer? A possible crash or getting blown up by an enemy shell?' 'Neither, if possible, but if choice is a must, preference is for crash', I said. 'Precisely. For that reason only, I am flying low', he said.

For the next one hour or so, we remained in the sky like the proverbial dove between the hunter and the falcon or, to put it bluntly, between life and death. As we moved further, I saw the aircraft struggling like a leaf tossed in a storm due to air pockets on the flight path. Unmindful of the shake-up frightening others,

I saw the pilot, cool and steady on his controls, manoeuvring the aircraft through the turbulence and listening to commands and warnings from ATCs of other airfields. Perhaps he had no time to think of anything else.

Confused thoughts passed through my mind during that one hour. Yes, Balakrishnan, you were on cloud nine when you got the Army Commission. You imagined yourself in the role of a 'Captain Marvel' in military uniform. Here is the time for action. You are in the skies now. You do not know what is going to happen the next minute. Will you be blown up in the air? No, that possibility is ruled out because the pilot has taken adequate care to avoid it. But then, will you crash on the ground? Possible. The pilot did not rule it out.

Then came the thought of what would happen after such a mishap. The whole thing moving in the air being reduced to a fireball in the blink of an eye; all materials, broken and bent, scattered all over the places; Charred human bodies, difficult to identify. Whatever can be picked up will be put in coffins and carried to the crematorium in a procession that will end up with a speech by a politician praising the unknown 'brave soldiers' for laying down their lives for the sake of the country, accompanied possibly by Lata Mangeshkar's song '*Zara ankh mein bharlo pani, Zara yaad karo kurbani*' in the background. Cremation will be with full military honours, with reverse arms and bugle sounding the last post. Quite impressive!

But what of my mother, for whom I am the only son and hope in life? Will she survive after the news reaches her? What about my wife who married me a year back? She will become a widow even before she knew what married life meant.

But for these thoughts, I would have enjoyed the panoramic view of Rajasthan desert which was unfolding part by part as the flight progressed.

When I turned my eyes again on the pilot, I saw his beaming face. 'No need to fear about scrambles now. We have crossed the danger zone', he said. 'So you will pull up now?' I enquired. 'Not necessary. In a short while from now, we will be steadying for landing', was his reply.

We landed safely. By evening the operation of ferrying the troop was completed without any mishap. I thanked the pilots and crew for their cooperation and went into the operational role allotted to me immediately.

Encounter with Thakazhi

A chance meeting with the well-known novelist and *Jnanapeeth* Award winner, Takazhi Shivashankara Pillai, is one of the incidents that come to my mind whenever I go into a recollection mode.

In my official capacity, I had some contact with customs authorities at Mumbai International Airport, and I used to make use of that for customs clearance of friends coming from abroad. Meeting with Thakazhi took place on one of those occasions.

I was waiting for my friend coming from Dubai in the customs area of the airport. As soon as he reached the area, I spotted him and showed him to the customs officer for speedy clearance. When the officer was about to take up his baggage for checking, my friend came to me and asked me whether it would be possible for me to extend similar help to another person. That other person was none other than Thakazhi.

Thakazhi had gone abroad to visit his daughter and was on his way back. He was in the same flight with my friend from Dubai. The frail old man in dhothi and half-shirt moving in the aisle of the aircraft with his unsteady gait could easily be identified as a Keralite returning home after his maiden foreign travel. My friend had heard about Thakazhi but had never seen him before.

Seeing the uneasy and nervous behaviour of this man, my friend approached him and asked him in Malayalam whether he needed any help.

Thakazhi took him into confidence straightaway and narrated his problems. He was very much worried about customs clearance at Mumbai International Airport because he had heard from his friends that customs authorities were very rude, and passengers were harassed and made to wait in queue for long time. Moreover, his air ticket for the connecting domestic flight from Mumbai to Thiruvananthapuram had not been confirmed. He had none to help him. My friend asked him whether he was carrying any article that would attract seizure or imposition of penalty by customs authorities. What he disclosed as contents of his baggage, both unaccompanied and hand luggage, did not appear to my friend as of any consequence from the customs angle.

It was from his talks that my friend made out that it was Thakazhi. My friend was very hesitant to ask me for help because he knew that nobody would willingly undertake such a job, particularly for a stranger. Yet he took the liberty of asking me not only because of the reputation Takazhi had in the literary field but also because of his old age and simplicity. I was hesitant because I was not sure how the customs officer would react to my request.

The customs officer who was clearing my friend happened to be a Keralite. That was a factor which emboldened me to approach him with a fresh request. When I asked him whether he could clear Thakazhi also as a favour to me, the officer smilingly nodded and asked my friend to bring Takazhi straight to his counter. When Thakazhi came to the counter, the officer politely requested him to be seated and cleared him along with my friend without even asking him to open his baggage. Thakazhi thus came out of the first round successfully, completely surprised of course, but with no sign of it on his face.

By the time we came out of the airport, it was already three in the morning. Takazhi had to proceed to the domestic terminal to catch his connecting flight to Tiruvananthapuram leaving at five in the morning. The domestic terminal was about two kilometres away from the international terminal by road. My friend had to be taken to a hotel nearby where he had booked a room. We decided that we would give Thakazhi a lift in our vehicle up to the domestic terminal before proceeding to the hotel as it would be difficult for him to get a taxi at that time. While proceeding to the domestic terminal, my friend told me that Thakazhi had only an unconfirmed ticket for the flight. That meant he would definitely get stranded at the airport since it was difficult in those days to get a seat unless you had booked much in advance. He had no idea or plan for the next step.

I could not think of leaving him at the airport and going away. After taking him to the departure lounge and making him sit, I went through the back door and managed a seat for him with the help of the duty officer of Indian Airlines who was fortunately known to me. After booking him on the flight, I handed over his ticket, baggage coupon and boarding pass to him. I saw a thin smile on his face which suggested to me that his tension had disappeared. Two or three Keralite youngsters who had confirmed seats on the same flight spotted Thakazhi and came to him after their booking formalities were completed. I requested them to take care of Thakazhi during the flight, and they readily agreed.

But his problems were still not over. He wanted a 'Kattan kaappi' (black coffee) and a 'beedi' (a country smoking device), the usual companions for most Keralites at daybreak in those days. I managed to get a cup of coffee without milk from the restaurant inside the airport, but beedi was out of question as it was not available in or near the airport. I offered my cigarette packet in lieu, but he declined it with a smile saying he only smoked beedi. He had to go without a smoke.

When security check was announced, I got up and escorted him up to the gate. When I said goodbye to him, he said, in a slow and measured tone, that what I had done for him might be God's reward for his lifelong service to Malayalam literature. I nodded with a smile.

I joined my friend who was patiently waiting in the vehicle parked in the parking area outside the airport. It was seven in the morning when I reached home after dropping my friend at the hotel.

Sahayak Waidande

I was travelling from Mumbai to Kerala by road. It must have been some time in the 1980s. I do not recollect the exact year, month and date now. I reached Karad, a small town ahead of Satara in the Western Ghat region of Maharashtra, by about half past four in the evening. As it was my evening tea time, I got out of the car and looked for a reasonably good teashop to have a good cup of tea and possibly some snacks. I wandered through the dusty lanes of that small town for quite some time. Since I could not locate one of acceptable standards, I decided to proceed further and look for one in the next town Kolhapur, which was about two hours drive from Karad.

While trekking back to my car, I noticed a policeman coming towards me. He was well turned out and he attracted my attention. Stopping in front of me, about six feet away, he came to attention and gave a smart salute. I was taken aback. *'Muje pehchana nahi Saab? Main Waidande hoon'* (Don't you recognise me, sir? I am Waidande). He introduced himself with a smile on his face as he saw me a bit confused. Yes, it was undoubtedly Vinayak Waidande, my Sahayak (known as 'orderly' or 'batman' before the term 'sahayak' replaced it) in my first unit.

Whenever I recollect my experiences during the India-Pakistan War of 1965, Waidande's name invariably comes to my mind.

At the outbreak of the war, my unit located in the southern part of the country was moved to the front by rail. The special train carrying men, equipment and stores, running at 'white hot' priority, reached the railway station near our expected operational area in two days. As per orders from higher formation, we disembarked at that station and moved into a nearby camp site with our equipment and stores. It was a readymade camp site with trenches all around and plenty of trees giving it a good camouflage.

Next day we were quite busy preparing for deployment of our troops in the area allotted to us. I was given certain duties by the Commanding Officer which involved moving around quite a bit, meeting concerned authorities etc. I left the camp early morning, and it took almost the whole day to complete the duties assigned to me.

When I came back to the camp, it was almost six in the evening. The sentry at the entrance halted me and requested me to get into a trench immediately as the camp was under enemy shelling. To the driver of my vehicle his instruction was to leave the vehicle in the camouflaged parking area and get into a trench as quickly as possible. Within minutes, we both were in the trench. Sporadic shelling was going on.

Like a rat, I moved through the well-laid-out trenches in the direction of the headquarters with the intention of meeting the Commanding Officer and giving my report on what I had done during the day. When I was negotiating a winding curve, a soldier who recognised me greeted me, and I responded in the usual army style. Immediately after that, I saw in the faint light a figure jumping out of a neighbouring trench and dashing towards me. He jumped into my trench and said '*Sab, main aapka khana leke ayaa* (Sir, I brought your food)'.

It was Waidande. He had seen me leaving the camp in the morning. I was not there for lunch or evening tea. Hoping that I would be back by evening, he collected packed dinner from the officers' mess and was waiting for me in the trench leading to the headquarters. He heard my voice when I was responding to the soldier's greetings and ran to catch up with me. I thanked him and accepted the dinner packet.

Waidande guided me to the headquarters which was housed in an underground chamber. There I met the Commanding Officer. After giving him my report, I took orders for the next day and moved to my underground troop headquarters along with Waidande.

While taking dinner, thoughts about Waidande came to my mind. He ran out in the open when shelling was going on and everyone was taking shelter in the trench. He was more concerned with my dinner than his own safety. What a crazy fellow!

Waidande accompanied me like Robinson Crusoe's Man Friday wherever I moved during the war. The war was over in two weeks, and troops deployed for the war were pulled out and moved to locations decided by Army Headquarters. I left the unit on my posting to another unit, and lost contact with Waidande.

All these thoughts passed through my mind when I met Waidande that evening. He took me to a decent Uduppi restaurant in the heart of the town and entertained me with a cup of tea and snacks.

During our talk at the restaurant, I learned that after his release from the army, he joined the Maharashtra State Police as a constable. He was posted at Karad a year ago. His native village was about four kilometres away from Karad. In recognition of his military service, he was allotted three acres of land by the Maharashtra Government in his native village which he converted into an agricultural farm. His wife and two school-going children were with him in Karad. He invited me to his house but I had to decline the invitation. It was already 5.30 pm and if I delayed my onward journey further, it would be very late by the time I reached Belgaum, the planned place of halt for the night. So we parted, and I continued my journey.

Waidande always comes to my mind as the epitome of sincerity, loyalty, and devotion to duty. Soldiers like Waidande make the Indian Army great.

Sukumaran and His Vices

'For a Rajput warrior, there are three things above everything else – his horse, his sword and his honour'. So wrote a historian while describing Rajput chivalry. We read ballads of Rajput warriors with great admiration during our school days, and their memories are still fresh in our minds. I was reminded of this memorable dictum in a different context on a later day. That was when I came in contact with a person by name Sukumaran who also had three main attractions in life – wine, tobacco, and women, all three considered 'major' vices in our part of the world. The first two became obvious at first sight, and the third one after closer contact. According to a common acquaintance, a failed romance in early life seems to have pushed Sukumaran into this waywardness.

He was past thirty when I met him first. He was staying in a bachelor's lodge then. Our acquaintance grew slowly, with occasional meetings along with friends. The relationship was good, and I found him an amiable person. Normally he was a quiet person but after a couple of drinks he would be in his element cracking jokes and indulging in 'philosophical talks'.

One day when I was alone with him, I took the liberty of asking him why he did not think of marriage. His quick response was 'Why own a cow when milk is available in plenty?' This was the philosophy of a frustrated and cynical person, I felt. I went a step further and said he would need someone to look after him in his old age. 'Why, any number of home nurses' was his rejoinder.

Once when I met him, he was coughing badly. The ash tray on the peg table was filled to the brim with cigarette stubs. Looking at it I jokingly said: 'nearer to lung cancer'. Coming out of the cough and breathing freely for some time, he asked me: 'Do you think lung cancer is the monopoly of smokers? Did not Winston Churchill, in spite of his devoted smoking, live a long and healthy life without any lung problem?' 'Well said, Suku, you are a genius', I complimented him smilingly.

Another time, I found him arguing with his lodge mate. I did not interfere, and left him saying 'hello'. Later on, his lodge mate told me that Suku was overstuffed that day, and it was his habit to get into an argumentative mood whenever he had a 'more than usual' dose.

Next time I met him, I asked him whether there was any instance of his losing self-control after a drinking session. 'Never' he said, adding 'I am careful to keep it within limits'. And what was that limit? 'O! Just two. Maximum three' was his reply. I teased him, saying: 'Only if you exceed that limit you get into an arguing mood, I suppose'. He countered saying, 'drinks have nothing to do with that'. 'God save your liver' I quipped. 'He won't have to do it. I can take care of that myself' was his reply. After a pause, he asked me: 'Haven't you heard of any case where non-alcoholics had cirrhosis of liver?' I just looked blank.

He had sound explanations for all these so-called 'vices'. I never touched upon the third 'vice' because of my fear of being beaten hollow with his cynical arguments.

He was a square peg in a round hole with subordinates, colleagues and superiors in his office as I learned from his colleague. Everyone was careful while dealing with him. He could survive because his was a government job and he was a permanent employee. Moreover, he was quite proficient in his work.

Never once during my acquaintance with him did I hear him uttering the name of God. Quite natural for a cynic like him.

It was after a long gap that I met him again. We both had turned grey but hair dye had helped him to conceal his age to some extent. It took some time for us to recognise each other. He was quite happy, and smelling of liquor and tobacco as usual. He was going to the bank to draw his pension. He said with a smile: 'Some people get pension to live, but I live to get pension'. When I looked at his dyed hair intently, he read my mind quickly and, without waiting for a comment from me, said: 'Why look old when you can look young?'

'Still going strong', I commented. While exchanging pleasantries, I casually asked: 'What about the old game?' He understood what I meant and shot back: 'at this age?' After a pause, he looked at me with a grin on his face and said 'no appetite'.

From his talks, I learned that he was living in a rented house nearby after retirement, and the pension he was getting was sufficient for a modest living which of course included the luxury of drinking and smoking although on a subdued scale. No liabilities or obligations.

We parted wishing good luck to each other.

Whenever I think of Sukumaran, Somerset Maugham's *Ant and the Grasshopper* story comes to my mind. In spite of his Bohemian lifestyle, he managed to survive with a smile on his face like Maugham's hero. Unfinished Problems like children's education, daughter's marriage, ailments associated with old age etc which pester most people following traditional ways, at the fag end of their life, were not there for him. He was more comfortably placed for an invitation from the land of no return than any other person.

But then, is it a life worthy of emulation? It does not appear so. Sukumaran's way of life was not based on any ideological or philosophical precepts but on his negative reactions arising, most likely, from frustrating and disappointing experiences in life. He may have been putting on a smiling face, but beneath that smile could be a feeling of loneliness and dejection. This cross-current also comes to my mind when I think of Sukumaran.

The Bomb Blast

During the India-Pakistan War of 1965, the Air Defence Regiment to which I belonged had its operational role in the north-western sector. Giving air defence cover to an airfield in Rajasthan sector was one of its tasks, and I was in the sub-unit detailed for this task. That airfield happened to be a target for Pakistani bombing.

As in the case of other operational airfields, bombing was confined to nights as daytime raids were impossible because of interception by our fighters. Due to total blackout at night, seldom could bombers get on to their intended targets correctly, and, consequently, bombing was inaccurate. Our air defence guns were World War II make without radar assistance, and we had, therefore, to resort to box or umbrella type barrage fire at night. Our operation was quite effective in preventing bombers from flying low and locating targets in faint light.

My duties were at the Command Post (CP). Directing air defence operations during bombing was the main duty at the CP. Two or three days went by, and the bombing operations seen in those days gave us some valuable ideas about enemy tactics. Attack was only after moonrise which indicated that the pilot was depending on moonlight for navigation. Moonrise thereafter became a part of our warning system. Next was that the pilot followed the railway track for guidance during flight from take off point to the target. That gave us a clue about his direction of approach. Strangely, another group of informants also gave us early warning – peacocks of the desert. Their crowing *en masse*, probably heralding moonrise, was another signal.

The Commanding Officer (CO) and Second-in-Command (2IC) of the Regiment visited our unit on one of those days. On their way, they received secret information about a possible sabotaging activity that night in the area where one of our troops was deployed. When they reached our location, it was about five in the evening. After meeting the Battery Commander (BC), they decided that I should take over that troop because the officer in charge of that troop was a young officer without much experience. The BC was to oversee the operations at the CP till I came back the next day.

I left the CP and went straight to the troop headquarters (Tp HQ), reaching the location by about six in the evening. After meeting the officer in charge and his number two, a Junior Commissioned Officer (JCO), and briefing them on the situation, I visited all gun positions (GPs) and briefed those manning the posts to ensure that they were on high alert. I came back to the Tp HQ by about nine at night and checked the line and radio communication with the CP and GPs to satisfy myself that they were in proper working condition. The operators were told to keep constant touch with the GPs and ascertain the situation at regular intervals. The sabotaging plan apparently fizzled out. Nothing untoward happened that night.

Moonrise was at about twelve that night. As usual, the peacocks began to crow *enmasse* when golden light began to appear on the eastern horizon. Our GPs were alerted, and we communicated our readiness in response to the 'report readiness' call from the CP.

Air-raid warning sirens of the Civil Defence Organisation sounded in another fifteen minutes. It was followed by announcement over mike directing civilians to move into trenches. Civil organisations like the Home Guards, Civil Defence and Fire Brigade would get their information from the railway network. As soon as the first railway station on the route sited a low-flying aircraft over it, the message would be flashed to the Railway Headquarters, which then would pass on the information to the concerned civil authorities. The system worked well and helped to minimise civilian casualties during bombing.

After another ten minutes, the sound of the aircraft became audible. About ten or fifteen nautical miles away from the area, the pilot pulled up to a safe height to avoid getting caught in the 'ack-ack' fire.

When the aircraft entered our defended area, order came from the CP to open fire, and all the guns started firing according to plan. It was a fantastic display of fireworks in the sky with shells bursting all around. The pilot made a dry run first to make sure that the flight was over the target area. After circling round, he came back aligning the aircraft approximately with the runway. He dropped a bomb this time, but it missed the mark and exploded outside the airfield. He made another sortie and dropped one more bomb. From my trench, I could see the explosion of this bomb with red and orange flames shooting up to about three hundred feet. It was seen in the direction of our CP. I tried to contact the CP through our communication network to ascertain where the bomb fell. There was no response from the other end.

The aircraft flew away after this sortie, and a few minutes later came the 'all clear' siren. I dashed to the nearby Air Force Signal Unit to see whether I could get any information about the place where the bomb fell. I was shocked to learn that the bomb fell in the corner of the airfield where our CP was located.

I came back to the Tp HQ thinking about the next step for me. First I thought of going to the CP immediately but then I gave up that plan since it would be incorrect to leave the Tp HQ at that time. The possibility of another raid or sabotaging activity before dawn could not be ruled out. So I decided to wait till morning.

Early morning next day, I went to the CP only to see it in shambles and totally deserted. There was no one nearby. I went to the Air Force Control Room which was about five hundred yards away. It was there that I got a complete picture of what happened the previous night. The bomb fell about a hundred yards away from the CP. The vibration following the explosion blew away the top of the CP, and sandbags stacked around came down virtually burying all inmates. No assistance could reach till the 'all clear' siren sounded. Rescue operation took more than an hour, and all inmates rescued were shifted to the Air Force Hospital immediately.

I proceeded to the Air Force Hospital where they were shifted after rescue. There I found the CO, 2IC, BC, CP JCO and two jawans in the intensive care unit lying in a semi-conscious state with life support systems. 'Condition stable at present' was the only answer I could get for my query from the Air Force doctor on duty.

The matter was reported to higher formation, and we were assured of immediate replacements. Till they reached, I was ordered to carry on with whatever assistance I could get from the Air Force authorities. I called for a meeting of the officers and JCOs of the Battery and briefed them. By evening, we activated the CP with men and equipment pulled out from the troops. Since radio sets were damaged we could think of line communication only, and with cables and a few field telephone sets arranged with Air Force assistance, we successfully established the communication network simultaneously.

For the next two nights, luckily there were no raids. Apparently, the raids were diverted to another airfield which was assumed by the enemy to be operationally active. Raid was resumed on the third day, but by that time, moon light had become faint and unhelpful to the pilot. This time we decided not to open fire during the dry run and waited for the pilot to come back aligning the aircraft with the runway. But that did not happen. The pilot seems to have got confused because he did not face any ack-ack fire on entry, and, after circling once or twice, he left the area probably thinking that he had either drifted on his course or had overshot. I saw an explosion far away from the airfield after some time which suggested to me that he had dropped bombs somewhere else mistaking it to be the target. There were no more raids, and the war ended four days later.

All the victims of the air raid survived. But the CO developed heart problems and was medically boarded out. The 2IC suffered from perforation of eardrums. Others had injuries all over their bodies. It took some time for them to come out of the trauma they had gone through.

Whenever I recollect this incident, the hospital scene comes to my mind first. It was a devastating experience – people with whom you were moving like family members till the previous day being seen lying like corpses the next day. A sure sight to make a person lose self-control. And then comes the thought I had immediately after this incident. What would have happened to me if the CO had not decided to send me away from the CP on the basis of the secret information?

When my unit got orders to move, I scribbled two letters, one to my wife and the other to my mother, saying that I was moving to the front. I could not say where to, since I did not know our destination till we reached Delhi. After that I did not get time to write any letters. There was no easy communication system in those days as we have today.

They did not know what was happening to me. They had no information other than what the All India Radio or newspapers gave about the war going on between India and Pakistan. As I came to know from my wife later, each time the telegraph messenger passed by the house sounding his bell, particularly at night, she and her family members would close their eyes and go into a prayer mode, coming back to normalcy only after the messenger went past the house. They lived on the assurance given by the astrologer that 'even though I was passing through the worst of times, I would come back intact'. And my wife would convey to my mother that everything was ok with me.

The Panda and I

When the word 'panda' is mentioned, it is possible that it would be taken as referring to that cute little animal seen in the zoo or at times on TV channels. I am referring not to that panda but to people seen in the temple complex at Nasik, a town located on the banks of River Godavari in Maharashtra. These people also are known by that name, and they are considered specialists in the art of providing assistance to departed souls seeking salvation. Their language and appearance would suggest a North Indian origin, and their ability to chant sacred verses (*mantra*) speaks of their priestly connection.

When my father died, elders assembled for cremation advised me that his ash collected on the third day after cremation (*sanjayanam*) should be immersed in water at a holy place like Rameshwaram or Kashi. Nasik was another place where this could be done, as I understood from friends. Like Ganga and Yamuna, Godavari is a sacred river for the Hindus. Moreover, this place was sanctified by the presence of Sage Agastya, according to the epic *Ramayana*. Rama and Seetha seem to have spent some days at Panchavadi near Nasik during their self-imposed exile (*vanavas*). It was also closer to my place of duty. All these factors made me choose Nasik to perform the ritual.

The moment I landed up at the temple complex, a pack of pandas, dressed like jokers in a circus with coats and caps over their traditional dress, swarmed around me, each promising better service than the other. I could not make out what they meant by the term 'better service'. I picked up one out of the lot for the simple reason that he looked cleaner than the rest.

'What is your wage?' I enquired. 'You mean *Dakshina*, Sir? Whatever you feel like giving'. That was his readymade answer. I was satisfied. He wanted me to change into a *dhoti* since the ritual could be performed only in the traditional dress. Since I did not carry a *dhoti* with me, I asked him where I could get one. He said he could provide it. When I asked him the cost, his reply was 'only twenty rupees, Sir'. So cheap! What an honest man! I felt.

As directed by him, I walked into the shallow water attired in that traditional outfit, and readied myself for the ritual standing in knee-deep water and holding the urn containing my father's ash above my head. He sat on a dais on the bank of the river about two metres away. I was asked to tell my name, my father's name and my '*gothra*' (lineage). For the first two, there was no problem. But the third one is an unknown factor for a Keralite Nair. Just for the sake of an answer, I said 'Nair', a term that did not figure in his directory of *gothra*. Without asking any further questions on this, he downgraded me to the status of a *shudra* (a low caste) with the tag 'Valmiki'. Since I have no caste prejudice, I did not mind it. In fact, I felt flattered when I got the tag Valmiki attached to me. It is indeed an honour to have lineage from a great person like Sage Valmiki, author of the epic *Ramayana*.

He then asked me to repeat what he chanted. After invoking the blessings of all imaginable Gods and demigods, a routine procedure in most rituals, he began to recount all possible sins and omissions my father would have committed during his lifetime, giving a pause in between for me to repeat what he said. My father was a simple and straightforward man and, as far as I knew him, was incapable of committing any of the sins he was being accused of. I felt outraged to see such unwarranted charges being levelled against him, and, after some time, my repetition of what he said became nothing more than mere noise.

Halfway through, I found him suddenly becoming serious in his chanting. He told me to listen carefully to what he was going to chant and repeat it without any mistake. I thought he was going to ask God to forgive my father for all the sins he had committed knowingly or unknowingly and felt that I must take it seriously.

After I nodded, communicating my acceptance, he began his new narrative. In a poetic form, he started: 'In expiation of the sins committed by my father, I, his son, shall gift a thousand and one cows to the Brahmin'. I did not repeat but stared into his eyes. Of course, he would have known that no sensible person would agree to such a fantastic proposal. Straightaway, he scaled down from his one thousand and one to one hundred and one to eleven and finally to one cow or its money equivalent. 'Hundred and one rupees' I said. 'What is a hundred and one rupees these days, Sir?' was his rejoinder. I pretended as though I had not heard him.

He concluded the ritual abruptly and directed me to come back from the river after throwing the urn behind me. I respectfully placed the urn on the flowing water and stood with folded hands till it floated away in running water. When I came back and paid him the amount promised, he took it with a wry face. He then asked me for the *dhoti* which he gave me for twenty rupees saying that it was the custom to donate it to a Brahmin after the ritual. I was only too happy to shed that unwanted cloth. He made twenty rupees that way too.

On my way back, thoughts about that panda came to my mind. What a clever man! He posed as an honest John in the beginning. That appeared to be only his business trick. To survive in a competitive world, these types of gimmicks would be necessary. He knew that if he had kept his demands high, people would avoid him and approach someone else who would be prepared to undercut. And he knew how to make his way through at the right time. People perform such rituals out of love and respect for the departed, and they may not mind spending money for them even if it be a bit lavish. At the right time, he would play his trump card, and gullible people would walk into his trap, if not for one thousand and one cows, at least for a comfortable amount.

I had never seen my father going to a temple; nor did I hear him uttering the name of God any time. That was in contrast to my mother who believed in God and was a devotee of the deity in the nearby temple. I was brought up in a liberal atmosphere, and, as I grew up, I moved closer to atheism under the influence of Marxist ideas. I went to Nasik to perform the ritual not because I believed in it but in deference to the wishes expressed by seniors. Not that I disrespected my father, but I did not believe in ideas like salvation. And I am sure my father also had no belief in such ideas. I was glad I did not get caught in that panda's net.

The Imposter

Recollections of my army days would be incomplete if I do not mention an interesting incident that took place during those days.

The event occurred during my days in a Regiment after the 1971 India-Pakistan War. I was the Adjutant (officer in charge, Administration) of the Regiment. After the games parade in the afternoon, it was my normal practice to visit my office to see whether there were any important letters or messages in the mail.

One day, after perusal of the mail, I was standing outside my cabin and talking to my Subedar Head Clerk. I saw a chauffeur-driven civilian car coming and halting in the car park a hundred yards away from my office. A person in army uniform got down from the car and walked towards my office after confirming the location of the Adjutant's office from the sentry standing nearby. As he came nearer, I could make out from his uniform and badges of rank that he was a Major from the Corps of Electrical and Mechanical Engineers (EME). He greeted me in the usual army style and introduced himself as Major Hassan from Army Headquarters, EME Directorate. I reciprocated and, after introducing myself, took him to my office.

When I asked him politely whether there was anything I could do for him, he smiled and said: 'Thanks. Nothing in

"

particular. I have come to the station to spend a few days with a relative of mine. This is only a courtesy call'. I thanked him for his kind gesture.

I asked him whether he would like to have a cup of tea. 'No, thanks. I already had tea before I came' was his reply. To my question whether his stay in the station was comfortable, his answer was: 'Of course, yes. I am staying with Majrooh Sultanpuri, the cine artist. He is a cousin of mine. That car you see there is his. I am able to move around freely because of that chauffeur-driven car'.

And that set the tone for the next stage in the conversation. 'You know, these filmi guys are a funny lot. Partying is an important part of their celluloid life. Yesterday there was a late-night party. I attended. Asha Parekh was the cynosure of all eyes'. He paused to see my reaction. Since he did not notice much enthusiasm in me, he did not pursue that topic.

'Where was your Regiment deployed during the recent war?' He asked. I said 'In the western sector'. 'Not much action, I suppose' was his comment. 'You are right, Sir' I said. 'I was in the eastern front' he continued. 'You see, I was almost knocked off'. Saying this, he got up, unbuttoned the lower portion of his shirt and showed me the mark of a healed cut on his stomach. 'A bullet tore through my belly' he said, adding 'It was a miracle that I survived. I was in the hospital for over four months, and now I am placed in the low category'. That, of course, was a matter to be taken seriously. He saw me quite receptive to his talks. You are lucky, Sir'. That was my response. He looked at his wristwatch and said: 'Oh no, I won't trouble you with details'.

He sat for some more time. He made enquiries about the Commanding Officer and Second-in-Command, and said that time permitting, he would come the next day or the day after to pay his respects to them. He also went through other matters like family life and the officers' mess in the unit. He got up and began moving towards his car saying 'God willing, we meet again'. I escorted him up to the car and said 'Glad to have met you, Sir. Good night'.

This is only a gist of the conversation between us. During his talks, he was freely using jargons familiar to service personnel, and he never failed to have the word 'bloody' prefixed to his statements many a time, a weakness of 'military chaps'.

But with all that, a strange feeling was passing through my mind during the time I spent with him. He was a thin, short-statured man with a dark complexion. He appeared quite smart, but his overall behaviour and appearance gave the impression that he lacked officer-like qualities (OLQ). I was wondering how such a person could get through the Service Selection Board (SSB). Could be that, being a technical man, the SSB might not have gone through finer requirements minutely as it does in other cases. While talking, I found him becoming alert suddenly. He stopped talking and put his hand in his pocket to take out his identity card. When I said 'not necessary, Sir', he cooled down. Probably, he read my mind correctly and appeared to be responding to what he might have considered a 'searching look' in my eyes at times.

I went home and forgot the matter. The next afternoon, when I was relaxing after lunch, I saw the same car that I had seen the previous evening approaching my bungalow and halting in my portico. The same Major Hassan got down. He was accompanied by a young boy whom he introduced as Sultanpuri's son. He was in casual civil dress. In the services, people are very strict about etiquettes. No officer barges into another officer's house at odd times. I felt a little uneasy about the way he conducted himself. Even if there was an emergency, he could have contacted me on the intercom from my office and taken my permission before coming to my house.

He apologised for coming and disturbing me at that time and said he had come to invite me for dinner at Sultanpuri's residence the next day evening. Of course, there would be film artists at the party. Normally, military people, particularly bachelors, are easily taken in by the mention of the 'tinsel world', but I had no great attraction for that. My experience taught me to be a little careful about the 'film world connection'. Invitation to parties in officers' mess is the main attraction for those 'glamorous' people, and that could be quite costly or even embarrassing sometimes.

I politely declined the invitation saying I was busy for the next two or three days. In spite of his repeated requests, I stuck to my stand. Then he asked me whether I could help him with some liquor for the party, of course, on cash payment. I expressed my inability to comply with his request, saying that I could not issue even a single bottle without the Commanding Officer's permission and that the CO was out of station. After taking a cup of tea with me, he left – a little disappointed, as I could make out from his face.

Two days later, I saw the same car on the road in front of my residence, this time heading towards the residence of the Officer in charge (OIC), EME Workshop, about a hundred yards away from my residence. It was about four in the afternoon, and I was getting out of my residence for the games parade. I went straight to the main gate and asked the sentry on duty whether he had checked that car and the identity of the occupant. The sentry answered in the affirmative and said he noticed no abnormality anywhere, including the identity of the officer sitting in the back seat (implying that he had checked his identity card also). Satisfied, I went for the parade. Major Hassan did not come to me that day or anytime thereafter.

A day or two later when I met the OIC, EME Workshop I asked him casually about the person who visited him without mentioning anything about my encounter with him. From his talk, I felt that he had not only no doubts about the person but was also feeling proud of his coming into contact with an army officer having close connection with film personalities. His daughter, a teenaged girl, was probably excited when she heard Major Hassan's talks about the film world and prevailed upon her father to encourage him. Thereafter, I saw Major Hassan visiting this officer a few times and taking him and his family out once or twice.

About two weeks went by, and he stopped coming. I took it that he must have returned to Delhi after his leave.

A month or so later, a police van came and stopped in the car park during office time. A police sub-inspector got out of the van and came to my office. He told me that a person who was seen moving around in a suspicious manner in a cantonment area was taken into custody by the military police and, being a civilian, was handed over to the civil police. During interrogation, that person disclosed that he had contacted two officers in my unit. The police officer's visit was to verify the facts. He requested me to follow him and have a look at the person he brought with him in the van.

When we reached the van, the police constable standing outside opened the door of the van. I was taken aback. The person whom the police brought in for my identification was none other than that 'Major Hassan' who met me a month back. He was in rags, handcuffed and seated between two police constables. Taking me slightly away from the van, the police officer asked me whether I recognised him. When I nodded, he asked me to narrate my experiences with him. When I completed, he smiled and said, 'Yes, in line with his recorded statement'. I asked the police officer about the identity card carried by that person. 'A fake card and a cleverly manipulated one too' was his reply. The police officer requested me to take him to the other officer mentioned by 'Major Hassan'. 'OK. Come along' I said and took him to the OIC Workshop.

The OIC Workshop became a little nervous when he heard that the person whom he entertained as 'Major Hassan' was a cheat. He did not want to meet the person brought by the police. When the police officer asked him some questions on the basis of the confessions made by 'Major Hassan', he could only say, 'I do not remember'. From the police officer's reaction, I felt that he had no intention to embarrass the OIC Workshop with unpleasant questions, and the questions he asked were meant only to show that he had done his duty.

When the police party was about to leave, I asked the police officer what the charges would be against this imposter. He said that no evidence had come up before the investigating team to implicate him in any espionage activity. Available evidence indicated that he was moving around army units posing as an army officer and trapping unsuspecting officers with his trump card of 'proximity to the film world'. According to his confession, he could entice quite a few officers in this way. They obliged him with liquor which he would sell to needy civilians at a premium.

Some of them even helped him financially. Next in the policy agenda, he said, was to go into his professed contact with film personalities. The charges would, in all probability, be cheating, impersonation, forging documents, etc.

I had no idea of what happened to him thereafter.

School Days

Primary Education (1935 to 1941)

When I was four years old, an elderly Kerala Brahmin (*Namboodiri*), whose name I do not recollect now, introduced me to the world of letters on *Vijaya Deshami* day by making me write the words '*Hari, Shree*' on rice filled in a bronze vessel with my right finger – a practice that continues to this day. Having thus qualified to start my education, I was taken to the nearby primary school, half a kilometre away from my residence, for enrolment in the infant class (known as KG class later). The person who escorted me to the school was Narayanan, a middle-aged man from my neighbourhood, under my mother's instruction.

When the teacher who enrolled me asked Narayanan my date of birth, he was unable to give it. All that he could tell was the star under which and the Malayalam month in which I was born which he had heard from my mother. The teacher worked out my date of birth on the basis of this information which was incorrect as I found out later. The difference was only a few days. I had to live with this error all through my life as I never attempted to correct it because of the elaborate procedure involved in it.

The school was under private management. Expenditure including salary of teachers was met from government grant. No amount was collected from students as fees. Teachers were poorly paid, and other than what the management gave them as salary once in two or three months, and that too a pittance, they had no income or benefits for their service. Many of them had to do odd jobs before and after school hours to make both ends meet.

It was difficult to get children to attend school in those days. Quite often, teachers had to go from house to house persuading parents to send their children to school to ensure that recognition given to the school was not withdrawn by government for want of minimum attendance. Parents at the lower levels of society were generally indifferent to their children's education, particularly that of girls. Students who were absent also would be marked present. No one would be detained in any class, even if performance was poor, because that would result in discontinuance of study or change of school.

During my time, total number of students in the school rarely exceeded sixty, of which girl students would have been about fifteen. Teaching staff including the headmaster would have been six or seven. There was no one to do clerical work. The headmaster himself did it I believe. No peon either, teachers doing whatever was normally done by peons in addition to their teaching work. There were no extracurricular activities in the school.

Students in the infant class had to sit on the floor and practice writing Malayalam alphabets on sand spread on the floor. Those who could afford a slate and pencil had the privilege of sitting on a bench and writing. I belonged to that category. All that was taught in the infant class was to write alphabets and pronounce them loudly. In the first standard, children moved on to writing and reading simple two or three-letter words and numbers. From that, the effort progressed to writing and reading simple sentences and children's story books in the second standard. From the third standard began the battle with English, and from the fourth, the trouble-makers – arithmetic and memorising tables.

Battle with tables was not so difficult, but with arithmetic it was different, particularly when it came to Mustafa's profit or loss in his grocery business. According to my reckoning, Mustafa should have closed down his business long ago as he had never made a profit. But no, Mustafa and his business continued to haunt me even after I moved to the secondary stage, not with the stock of rubber and pencil as at the primary stage but with tonnes of grains and pulses. Then I discovered that the fault lay not with Mustafa's business acumen but with my calculations which were going haywire all the time.

I was declared 'passed and eligible for secondary education' after I finished standard five in that school. I have a feeling that children of my time learned very little during their primary education stage compared to what a child of today learns at that stage.

Sometime after I left that school, management changed, and it became a society-managed institution. Its location also changed, and it continues today at the new site in a better and more organised form compared to what it was during my days, with ten times more children.

Secondary Education (1941 to 1947)

My father took me to the secondary school, about a kilometre away from my house, for enrolment in standard VI (known as 'first form' in those days) after I left the primary school. That was the only secondary school in that area in those days, and it was under private management. The headmaster admitted me in first form after satisfying himself that I could read a few lines from an English text book for standard V.

The school charged a fee of Rs 2.25 per month for the first three years and Rs 4.50 per month for the next three years. There were no uniforms for students. Boys wore trousers and half-sleeve shirts at the lower levels and trousers/dhotis and half-sleeve/folded full-sleeve shirts at the higher stage. Girls wore skirts and blouses at all levels.

Teachers wore dhoti and full-sleeve shirts and a 'mandatory' coat over the shirt. To be recognised as a 'man of standing' in those days (the colonial era), one should have 'saheb's dress' to some extent at least. When a person became a 'gazetted officer', he had to be in 'full suit' while on duty. Brahmin teachers with tuft had to put on a turban over the head to conceal the tuft. During my time, there was no lady teacher in the school.

Total number of students never exceeded three hundred, and girls constituted about ten percent of the total. Rich families being few, there were only very few students from well-to-do families. Boys belonging to the lower strata of society were shoved into the school by indifferent parents because of their nuisance value at home – most of them overage for the class and bad examples to younger students. Many would leave half way because of their indifference or inability of their parents to pay school fee.

There were only few Christian families in our area at that time, and Christian students attending the school were limited. Muslims, although large in number, were engaged mostly in trading activities and would start training their male children in that line from their early days. Because of this, Muslim boys were also few.

No Muslim girl could be seen attending any school, primary or secondary. Whatever they learnt from religious institutions (*madrassas*) at their young age was all that Muslim girls could speak of as their education. There was no encouragement for other girls too. Most parents would not take the 'risk' of sending their daughters outside their house once they attained puberty. Many girls who joined secondary schools would drop out at the age of twelve or thirteen because of restrictions from parents, and hardly three or four would reach the final stage. Girls and boys never talked to each other inside or outside the school.

The school suffered badly from mismanagement. It was receiving government grant, but that apparently went into the pockets of private management. Teachers, numbering about ten or twelve, were poorly paid and, like those of privately managed primary schools, had to look for other part-time jobs to carry on. Since the management had employed a clerk and a peon, they escaped doing clerical and menial jobs in addition to their teaching work.

Generally, teachers were an indifferent lot. The teacher who taught English in the first form was addicted to inhaling tobacco snuff. He would take a deep inhalation before entering the class, and teaching English language with his blocked nostrils would be disastrous. Another teacher, devoted to pan chewing, would come to the class with his pan-filled mouth.

Every five minutes, he would go out to spit, and that area near the classroom would become a veritable spittoon. The PT instructor, a man of poor health, would seldom get up from his chair during 'PT classes'. The Sanskrit 'pandit' never bothered to teach that language since it was only a 'secondary language'. The mathematics teacher would make sure that what he taught was never understood by students. That was his clever way of attracting students for his private tuition class. Only very few teachers commanded respect. There were no games, sports or extracurricular activities to speak of.

I was an average student, to begin with. If I liked a teacher, I would pay attention to what he taught, and performance in his subject would be satisfactory. There was nobody at home to guide me. This attitude, however, changed as I moved to higher levels. I worked hard and was able to make up, to a great extent, what I lost at the earlier stage. In the final Board examination, out of the forty five students (42 boys and three girls) who appeared, fourteen students were declared passed with two boys getting over fifty percent marks. I was one of those 'lucky' two.

I left the school in 1947, the year in which India became independent, to pursue my university education. A few years after I left, management of the school was taken over by a society. It continues in the same location today, with more buildings squeezed into the premises to accommodate the large number of students. Total number of students today may be about five times that of my time. Boys and girls from Christian and Muslim communities have also started joining the school in large numbers. About ten more secondary schools have come up in the region, and there is stiff competition between the schools for excellence. Performance of the school improved greatly after the management changed.

Life in General

Reminiscences of my school days would be incomplete without an observation on the general conditions prevailing in the village at that time.

Population of the region (the town and surrounding villages), according to a rough estimate, would have been about ten thousand in the 1940s. Hindus were in the majority. Then came Muslims. Christians constituted a small minority. Both Muslims and Christians were descendants of converts from lowcaste Hindus, conversion having taken place long back.

Hindus were highly caste-conscious. In fact, each person's name would have the caste name prefixed or suffixed to it as a mark of identity. Upper castes ill-treated lower castes. The former never entertained the latter in their houses, never sat and ate together with them. Inter-caste marriage was unheard of. Lower castes were denied entry into Hindu temples. Each lower caste group had its own place for common worship, and deities in those places would generally be of non-Aryan tradition. Quite often, those Gods had to identify with Hindu Gods to avoid extinction because of the presence of 'more powerful' Hindu Gods nearby.

People had nothing but their customs and traditions to guide them, and hence tended to be conservative in their outlook. Literacy would have been not more than fifty percent. Educated people were few, and those who succeeded in getting some jobs in government service because of their western-oriented education would try to be more English than the Englishmen themselves.

Medical facility was limited, and mortality rate, particularly among infants, very high. There was only one government hospital for the whole region, one doctor (a licensed medical practitioner) and one 'qualified' nurse. The doctor would be the 'specialist' for all branches of medicine, dentistry to gynaecology. People were in the habit of depending on quacks for treatment of diseases and that could be one reason for the high mortality rate.

Health care was in no way better. Every year, there would be a heavy toll on life due to deadly diseases like typhoid, smallpox and cholera. There was no treatment for these diseases in those days. Only a 'health inspector' went around 'vaccinating' people as a check on the spread of these infectious diseases. People considered those diseases the result of displeasure of their Gods and would go in for all sorts of occult practices to please them and save the village from such mishaps.

Communication with outside regions was very poor. Railway line on the Malabar Coast skirted the region, and the nearest railway station was about twelve kilometres away from the town. There were four rivers, two on the northern side and two on the southern side, within a radius of twenty kilometres from the centre of the town, and none of them had bridges over them. Private buses carried passengers in between the rivers, and they had to be ferried across the rivers in manned boats. Travelling time to reach places twenty-five kilometres away would be not less than three hours. Roads were in deplorable condition, dusty during dry season and slushy during rainy season. Cars, vans and motorcycles were a rare sight on the road. If a motorcycle appeared on the road facing the school, children would run to the gate to get a glimpse of this 'roaring' machine and its 'adventurous' rider.

Telephones, radio, television, electricity and banks were non-existent. A telegraph line was the only means to connect the region with the outside world. There was a Post and Telegraph Office in the town which would send or receive telegraphic messages. Sending or receiving letters and money orders and acting as a bank for money deposits were the other services provided by this office.

For domestic purposes, kerosene lamps were normally used. For night functions, including marriages, the 'petromax', an innovation on kerosene lamps to provide better light, would be used. Since there were no street lights, travelling at night would be quite hazardous, and hence, outside movements would generally thin out and cease after six in the evening. A person travelling at night had to depend on country-made torch (made of dry coconut leaves) for navigation through dark roads. Howling of jackals from neighbouring vacant plots and hooting of owls moving from treetop to treetop would pierce the silence of dark nights.

Economic life was on caste and community lines. Income of upper caste Hindus came mainly from tenancy-based landholdings. Lower caste men either followed their traditional professions such as weaving, pottery making, haircutting etc. or worked as manual labourers while their women did menial jobs in upper caste houses. Few upper caste educated men would manage to get employment under the colonial government or in educational institutions. Some engaged themselves in the legal/medical profession after taking a degree or diploma in law/medicine. Muslims were generally engaged in trade. People were poor, with many able-bodied men and women remaining unemployed or underemployed. Only a few families could be considered 'rich'.

Population being limited, land was a surplus commodity. Even an average middle class family owned an acre or two. The traditional upper class holdings ran into hundreds of acres. Most landholdings including agricultural land remained unutilised. Consequently, land value remained low.

Three Hindu temples and one mosque in the region addressed the religious needs of people. Of the three temples, two were dedicated to Shiva and one to Vishnu. The annual festival season (February-March) injected life into the otherwise dormant social atmosphere. That would be the time for brisk business for the trading community and social and cultural entertainment time for people as a whole. Touring cinema, circus and performing arts like drama and *kathakali* appeared during this season making it lively.

The 'gramophone' (old music system) was a status symbol for a house. It cost about a hundred and fifty rupees in those days, and only 'rich' people could afford it. It would provide added attraction for marriage functions, and for that, it could be hired for two rupees per programme from a shop dealing with musical instruments.

The Second World War (1939-45) brought about far-reaching social and economic changes. With the Japanese attack on Pearl Harbour, the War spread to the Far East, and Britain began strengthening the Indian Army fearing a Japanese attack on India. Large number of men in the age group 20-40, particularly those belonging to the lower levels of society, got enrolled in the army and moved out of the village. Interaction with outside world was of immense help in breaking their parochialism and conservatism. Their income helped to improve the financial condition of their families. Educational concessions announced by the colonial government to dependents of serving soldiers helped many families to send their children to schools and colleges. Rapid spread of Western-oriented education and improvement in financial conditions began to shake the foundations of the stagnant feudal society.

Efforts to mobilise resources during the war led to acute shortage in the consumer sector necessitating government intervention to ensure supply of essential commodities during the post-war period. This affected the traditional trade structure and became instrumental in providing incentive to increased production of consumer goods.

Another noticeable event was the emergence of political awareness among students during this period. 'Quit India' Resolution of 1942 and the arrests of political leaders that followed it produced a commotion all over the country. In the rallies and demonstrations organised in protest, students also began to participate. Soon, 'Student Unions' began to spring up in educational institutions, and discussions on political matters became a lively issue, particularly among senior students. Political leaders encouraged this development.

Hindu temples in which entry was restricted to upper-caste Hindus were thrown open to public removing caste consideration after India became independent. This step helped to reduce sharpness of the caste system and paved the way for inter-caste marriages subsequently. This was followed by 'land-to-the-tiller policy' and reforms in the field of education. They also helped to change the feudal character of society to a great extent.

University education and professional career took me away from my village in the 1950s. Sixty years later, when I came back to live my retired life in the same village, I found it completely changed in every respect.